D0982610

The Calendar and Collects

The Calendar and Collects

According to the use of
THE CHURCH OF IRELAND

By authority of the General Synod
of the Church of Ireland
2001

COLUMBA

the columba press

First published in 2001 by
The Columba Press
55a Spruce Avenue, Stillorgan Industrial Park,
Blackrock, Co Dublin

Designed by Bill Bolger
Origination by The Columba Press
Printed in Ireland by Betaprint Ltd, Dublin

ISBN 1 85607 355 6

Acknowledgements
Thanks are expressed to the following holders of copyright:
The Governing Body of the Church of Wales, for prayers from *The Book of Common Prayer*, © 1984; The Trustees of the Anglican Church of Australia, for prayers from *An Australian Prayer Book*, © 1978; The Provincial Trustees of the Church of the Province of South Africa, for prayers from *An Anglican Prayer Book*, © 1989; The Archbishops' Council of the Church of England, for prayers from *Common Worship*, © 2000, from *Promise of His Glory*, © 1990, and from *Lent, Holy Week and Easter*, © 1988, used by permission; The European Province of the Society of Saint Francis, for prayers from *Celebrating Common Prayer*, © 1991; Continuum International Publishing Group Ltd, for prayers from *After Communion* by Charles MacDonnell, © 1985, and for an original prayer by David Silk, © 1980, used by permission; Bishop Kenneth Stevenson; The Principal of Westcott House, Cambridge; The General Synod of the Anglican Church in Canada for prayers excerpted or adapted from the *Book of Alternative Services of the Anglican Church of Canada*, © 1985, used by permission; SPCK for prayers from *Enriching the Christian Year*, © 1993, and for a prayer by Janet Morley from *All Desires Known*, © 1992, used by permission of the publishers; The Church of the Province of New Zealand for prayers from *A New Zealand Prayer Book*, © 1988.

An attempt has been made to ascertain the copyright holders of other prayers. Where this has not been possible the sources have been indicated, and if any oversight has occurred this will be corrected when the Book of Common Prayer is published.

Contents

Introduction

In May 2001 the General Synod passed a statute, the contents of which form the Calendar and Collects for the new edition of the *Book of Common Prayer*. It was decided that this should come into force immediately because it relates to the lectionary already approved and the contemporary language collects and post communion prayers replace those issued for trial use in 1995. Services for the *Book of Common Prayer* 2004 so far approved will be authorised on publication of the book.

This book is being produced in the style chosen for the new edition of the *Book of Common Prayer*.

It has been possible to harmonise the Calendar in such a way that those who prefer to use the collects and readings of the 1926 edition can do so with very few alterations. These mostly relate to the Sundays designated 'Sundays before Advent' and 'Sundays before Lent', where the 1926 system of using the propers of Sundays after Epiphany to make up extra Sundays has been replaced. A table of readings is provided.

It is envisaged that where services are in both 16th/17th century style and 20th/21st century style, the former will be designated style 'One' and the latter style 'Two'. Thus, in this book collects in traditional language are designated 'Collect One' and those in contemporary language 'Collect Two'. At services in traditional language it is expected that Collect One will normally be used and Collect Two at services in contemporary language, but there is nothing mandatory in the statutes.

This book is issued to encourage the prayer of the church and to prepare for the exciting venture of a new edition of the book that has nourished the worship of the Church of Ireland for the four hundred and fifty years since the *Book of Common Prayer* was published in 1551.

The Calendar

All Sundays celebrate the paschal mystery of the death and resurrection of Christ. Nevertheless, they also reflect the character of the seasons in which they are set.

PRINCIPAL HOLY DAYS

The principal holy days which are to be observed are:

Christmas Day 25 December
Easter Day
The Day of Pentecost (Whitsunday)
On these days the Holy Communion is celebrated in every cathedral and parish church unless the ordinary shall otherwise direct.

The Epiphany 6 January
In any year where there is a Second Sunday of Christmas the Epiphany may be observed on that Sunday.

The Presentation of Christ 2 February
The Presentation of Christ may be observed on the Sunday falling between 28 January and 3 February.
Maundy Thursday

The Ascension Day
Trinity Sunday
All Saints' Day 1 November
All Saints' Day may be observed on the Sunday falling between 30 October and 5 November.

On these days it is fitting that the Holy Communion be celebrated in every cathedral and in each parish church or in a church within a parochial union or group of parishes.

Good Friday is also a principal holy day.

The liturgical provision for the above days may not be displaced by any other observance.

Advent

Four Sundays and weekdays preceding Christmas Day

Christmas

Christmas Day to the eve of the Epiphany

Epiphany

From the Epiphany to the Presentation of Christ

When 6 January is a Sunday the Festival of the Baptism of our Lord is observed on a weekday, and 13 January is the Second Sunday of Epiphany.

Lent

From Ash Wednesday to Easter Eve

Within Lent the last two weeks are commonly called Passiontide.

Easter

The Fifty Days from Easter Day to the Day of Pentecost

Within Eastertide no festival listed below may displace the celebration of Sunday as a memorial of the Resurrection.

Rogation Days are the three days before the Ascension Day, when prayer is offered for God's blessing on the fruits of the earth and human labour.

The nine days following the Ascension Day until Pentecost are days of prayer and preparation to celebrate the outpouring of the Spirit.

ORDINARY TIME

There are two parts of the year which are not included in seasons. In the first, from the day after the Presentation of Christ to Shrove Tuesday, Sundays are designated as Sundays before Lent, the number depending on the date of Easter. In the second, from the Monday after the Day of Pentecost to the Eve of Advent Sunday, Sundays are designated in relation to Trinity Sunday, the last five as Sundays before Advent.

DAYS OF SPECIAL OBSERVANCE

Ash Wednesday, the First Day of Lent

The Monday, Tuesday and Wednesday of Holy Week

Easter Eve

No celebration of a festival takes place during Holy Week.

Ash Wednesday

The other weekdays of Lent

All Fridays in the year except Christmas Day, The Epiphany, the Fridays following Christmas Day and Easter and festivals outside the season of Lent

FESTIVALS

The Naming and Circumcision of Jesus	1 January
The Baptism of our Lord *observed as the First Sunday of Epiphany*	
except when 6 January is a Sunday (see above)	
The Conversion of Saint Paul	25 January
Saint Brigid	1 February
Saint Patrick	17 March
Saint Joseph of Nazareth	19 March
The Annunciation of our Lord	25 March
Saint Mark the Evangelist	25 April
Saint Philip and Saint James, Apostles	1 May
Saint Matthias	14 May
The Visitation of the Blessed Virgin Mary	31 May
Saint Columba	9 June
Saint Barnabas	11 June
The Birth of Saint John the Baptist	24 June
Saint Peter	29 June
Saint Thomas	3 July
Saint Mary Magdalene	22 July
Saint James the Apostle	25 July
The Transfiguration of our Lord	6 August
Saint Bartholomew	24 August
The Birth of the Blessed Virgin Mary	8 September
Saint Matthew	21 September
Saint Michael and all Angels	29 September
Saint Philip the Deacon	11 October
Saint Luke	18 October
Saint James, the Brother of our Lord	23 October
Saint Simon and Saint Jud	28 October
The Kingship of Christ	*The Sunday before Advent*
Saint Andrew	30 November
Saint Stephen	26 December
Saint John the Evangelist	27 December
The Holy Innocents	28 December

Liturgical provision is made for the above days in this book.

Days of prayer for those ordained or preparing for ordination: the Wednesday, Friday and Saturday after the first Sunday in Lent, the day of Pentecost, 14 September and 13 December.

These may be varied by the ordinary to relate to times of ordination in the diocese.

RULES TO ORDER OBSERVANCE OF FESTIVALS

Festivals falling on a Sunday may be transferred to the following Monday or at the discretion of the minister to the next suitable weekday.

Festivals falling on the first Sunday of Christmas may be observed on that day or transferred to the next available weekday.

When Saint Patrick's Day falls on the Sixth Sunday of Lent or the Monday or Tuesday of Holy Week Saint Patrick's Day is observed on the previous Saturday. When Saint Patrick's Day falls on another Sunday of Lent it may be observed on the Sunday or on the previous Saturday or the following Monday.

When Saint Joseph's Day or the Annunciation of our Lord falls on a Sunday in Lent they are observed on the Monday following the Second Sunday of Easter or at the discretion of the minister on another suitable weekday in the same week.

When Saint Mark's Day falls in the first week of Easter it is observed on the Monday following the Second Sunday of Easter or at the discretion of the minister on another suitable weekday in the same week.

Festivals falling on a Sunday of Eastertide are observed on the Monday following or at the discretion of the minister on another suitable weekday in the same week.

Saint Columba's Day or Saint Barnabas' Day falling on Trinity Sunday are observed on the Monday following or at the discretion of the minister on another suitable weekday in the same week.

Festivals not covered by the above rules may be observed on the Sunday or on a suitable weekday in the same week.

A list of persons associated with dioceses of the Church in Ireland. Some are church founders, some as reformers and re-builders, some went as missionaries to carry the Gospel to other lands. Dates are those linked with their names; some are those of the anniversary of their deaths. These are included for reference and to remind us of the continuing work of the Holy Spirit in the Church in all ages. The post-Reformation 'worthies' included reflect the Church of Ireland's relationship with other parts of the Anglican Communion.

Munchin, abbot. Limerick diocese, 7th century	2 January
Edan, bishop, Ferns diocese, 632	31 January
BRIGID or Bríd, Abbess of Kildare. circa 525	1 February
Kieran of Seirkeiran. Ossory diocese. circa 545	5 March
PATRICK. 461	17 March
Maccartan, bishop. Clogher diocese. cia 505	24 March
Laserian, abbot. Leighlin diocese. 639	18 April
Assicus (or Tassach), bishop. Elphin diocese. 470	27 April
Comgall of Bangor, abbot. Down diocese. 602	10 May
Carthagh, bishop. Lismore diocese. 637	14 May
Brendan, the Navigator. Ardfert & Clonfert dioceses. 577	16 May
Kevin. Glendalough diocese. 618	3 June
Jarlath. Tuam diocese. circa 550	6 June
Colman. Dromore diocese. 6th century	7 June
COLUMBA. Abbot of Iona. 597	9 June
Richard Fitzralph, Archbishop of Armagh. 1360	27 June
Moninne of Killeavy. Armagh diocese. 518	6 July
Kilian, bishop and martyr. Kilmore diocese. 689	8 July
Declan of Ardmore, bishop. Cloyne diocese. 5th century	24 July
Felim. Kilmore diocese. circa 560	9 August
Crumnathy or Nathi. Achonry Diocese. circa.610	9 August
Muredach or Murtagh. Kilalla diocese. circa 480	12 August
Jeremy Taylor, Bishop of Down and Connor and Dromore. 1667	13 August
Fachtna (or Fachanan), bishop. Ross diocese. 6th century	14 August
Charles Inglis, Bishop in N. America from Raphoe. 1816	16 August
Oengus Mac Nisse of Dalriada. Connor diocese. 514	3 September
Ciaran of Clonmacnois. circa 545	9 September

Finnian of Movilla in the Ards. Down diocese. 579.	10 September
Ailbhe, bishop. Emly diocese. circa 526	12 September
Eunan, abbot. Raphoe diocese. 7th century	2 September
Fin Barre. Cork diocese. 623	25 September
Canice, bishop. Ossory diocese. 6th century	11 October
Móibhí, teacher. 545.	12 October
Gall, missionary. Down diocese. 630	16 October
Otteran, abbot. Waterford diocese. 563	27 October
Malachy, bishop. Armagh and Down dioceses. 1148	3 November
Laurence O'Toole. Dublin and Glendalough dioceses. 1180	14 November
Columbanus, abbot. Down diocese. 615	23 November
Colman. Cloyne diocese. 601.	24 November
Finnian of Clonard, abbot. Meath diocese. circa 549	12 December
Flannan. Killaloe diocese. 640	18 December

The Collects

The First Sunday of Advent

Almighty God, COLLECT ONE
Give us grace that we may cast away the works of darkness,
and put upon us the armour of light,
now in the time of this mortal life,
in which thy Son Jesus Christ
came to visit us in great humility;
that in the last day,
when he shall come again in his glorious Majesty
to judge both the quick and the dead,
we may rise to the life immortal;
through him who liveth and reigneth with thee
and the Holy Spirit, now and ever. Amen.

This Collect is said after the Collect of the day until Christmas Eve.

Almighty God, COLLECT TWO
Give us grace to cast away the works of darkness
and to put on the armour of light
now in the time of this mortal life
in which your Son Jesus Christ came to us in great humility;
that on the last day
when he shall come again in his glorious majesty
to judge the living and the dead,
we may rise to the life immortal;
through him who is alive and reigns with you and the Holy Spirit,
one God, now and for ever. 1#

God our deliverer, POST COMMUNION
Awaken our hearts
to prepare the way for the advent of your Son,
that, with minds purified by the grace of his coming,
we may serve you faithfully all our days;
through Jesus Christ our Lord. 4

The Second Sunday of Advent

O Lord,

COLLECT ONE

Raise up (we pray thee) thy power, and come among us,
and with great might succour us;
that whereas, through our sins and wickedness,
we are sore let and hindered
in running the race that is set before us,
thy bountiful grace and mercy
may speedily help and deliver us;
through the satisfaction of thy Son our Lord,
to whom with thee and the Holy Spirit,
be honour and glory, world without end. Advent 4 1926

Collect of 5th before Advent may be used.

Father in heaven,

COLLECT TWO

who sent your Son to redeem the world
and will send him again to be our judge:
Give us grace so to imitate him
in the humility and purity of his first coming
that when he comes again,
we may be ready to greet him
with joyful love and firm faith;
through Jesus Christ our Lord. 15#

Lord,

POST COMMUNION

here you have nourished us with the food of life.
Through our sharing in this holy sacrament
teach us to judge wisely earthly things
and to yearn for things heavenly.
We ask this through Jesus Christ our Lord. 20#

The Third Sunday of Advent

O Lord Jesu Christ,
who at thy first coming didst send thy messenger
to prepare thy way before thee;
Grant that the ministers and stewards of thy mysteries
may likewise so prepare and make ready thy way,
by turning the hearts of the disobedient to the wisdom of the just,
that at thy second coming to judge the world
we may be found an acceptable people in thy sight,
who livest and reignest with the Father and the Holy Spirit,
ever one God, world without end.

O Lord Jesus Christ,
who at your first coming sent your messenger
to prepare your way before you:
Grant that the ministers and stewards of your mysteries
may likewise so prepare and make ready your way
by turning the hearts of the disobedient to the wisdom of the just,
that at your second coming to judge the world
we may be found an acceptable people in your sight;
for you are alive and reign with the Father and the Holy Spirit,
one God, world without end. 1#

Father,
we give you thanks for these heavenly gifts.
Kindle us with the fire of your Spirit
that when Christ comes again
we may shine as lights before his face;
who is alive and reigns with you and the Holy Spirit,
one God, now and for ever. 4#

The Fourth Sunday of Advent

Lord, COLLECT ONE
we beseech thee, give ear to our prayers,
and by thy gracious visitation
lighten the darkness of our hearts
by our Lord Jesus Christ;
who liveth and reigneth with thee
and the Holy Spirit, one God, now and for ever. BCP 1549-1662

God our redeemer, COLLECT TWO
who prepared the blessed Virgin Mary
to be the mother of your Son:
Grant that, as she looked for his coming as our saviour,
so we may be ready to greet him
when he comes again as our judge;
who is alive and reigns with you and the Holy Spirit,
one God, now and for ever. 8#

Heavenly Father, POST COMMUNION
you have given us a pledge of eternal redemption.
Grant that we may always eagerly celebrate
the saving mystery of the incarnation of your Son.
We ask this through him whose coming is certain,
whose day draws near,
your Son Jesus Christ our Lord. 20#

Christmas

Christmas Eve

O God, COLLECT ONE
who makest us glad with the yearly remembrance
of the birth of thy only Son Jesus Christ;
Grant that, as we joyfully receive him for our Redeemer,
so we may with sure confidence,
behold him when he shall come to be our Judge,
who liveth and reigneth with thee and the Holy Spirit,
one God, world without end.

Almighty God, COLLECT TWO
you make us glad with the yearly remembrance
of the birth of your Son Jesus Christ:
Grant that, as we joyfully receive him as our redeemer,
we may with sure confidence behold him
when he shall come to be our judge;
who is alive and reigns with you and the Holy Spirit,
one God, now and for ever. 1#

God for whom we wait, POST COMMUNION
you feed us with the bread of eternal life:
Keep us ever watchful,
that we may be ready to stand before the Son of Man,
Jesus Christ our Lord. 16

The Nativity of our Lord (Night)

O God, COLLECT ONE
who madest this most holy night
to shine with the brightness of his coming,
who is the light of the world;
Grant that we who on earth hail the brightness of his appearing
may rejoice hereafter in the light of his heavenly glory;
who with thee and the Holy Spirit,
liveth and reigneth, one God, now and for ever. Indian BCP 1960

Eternal God, COLLECT TWO
who made this most holy night
to shine with the brightness of your one true light:
Bring us, who have known the revelation
of that light on earth,
to see the radiance of your heavenly glory;
through Jesus Christ our Lord. 2

God our Father. POST COMMUNION
in this night you have made known to us again
the power and coming of our Lord Jesus Christ:
Confirm our faith and fix our eyes on him
until the day dawns
and Christ the Morning Star rises in our hearts.
To him be glory both now and for ever. 8

Christmas Night **23**

The Nativity of our Lord (Day)

Almighty God, COLLECT ONE
who hast given us thy only-begotten Son
to take our nature upon him,
and as at this time to be born of a pure virgin;
Grant that we being regenerate,
and made thy children by adoption and grace,
may daily be renewed by thy Holy Spirit;
through the same our Lord Jesus Christ,
who liveth and reigneth with thee and the same Spirit,
ever one God, world without end.

Almighty God, COLLECT TWO
you have given us your only-begotten Son
to take our nature upon him
and as at this time to be born of a pure virgin:
Grant that we, who have been born again
and made your children by adoption and grace,
may daily be renewed by your Holy Spirit;
through Jesus Christ our Lord. 1#

God our Father, POST COMMUNION
whose Word has come among us
in the Holy Child of Bethlehem:
May the light of faith illumine our hearts
and shine in our words and deeds;
through him who is Christ the Lord. 16

The First Sunday of Christmas

Almighty God, COLLECT ONE
who hast given us thy only-begotten Son
to take our nature upon him,
and as at this time to be born of a pure virgin;
Grant that we being regenerate,
and made thy children by adoption and grace,
may daily be renewed by thy Holy Spirit;
through the same our Lord Jesus Christ,
who liveth and reigneth with thee and the same Spirit,
ever one God, world without end.

Almighty God, COLLECT TWO
who wonderfully created us in your own image
and yet more wonderfully restored us
through your Son Jesus Christ:
Grant that, as he came to share in our humanity,
so we may share the life of his divinity;
who is alive and reigns with you and the Holy Spirit,
one God, now and for ever. 7

Heavenly Father, POST COMMUNION
you have refreshed us with this heavenly sacrament.
As your Son came to live among us,
grant us grace to live our lives,
united in love and obedience,
as those who long to live with him in heaven;
through Jesus Christ our Lord. 24

The Second Sunday of Christmas

Almighty God,
who hast poured upon us the new light of thine incarnate Word;
Grant that the same light, enkindled in our hearts,
may shine forth in our lives;
through Jesus Christ our Lord.

Almighty God,
in the birth of your Son
you have poured on us the new light of your incarnate Word,
and shown us the fullness of your love:
Help us to walk in this light and dwell in his love
that we may know the fullness of his joy;
who is alive and reigns with you and the Holy Spirit,
one God, now and for ever. 2#

Light eternal, POST COMMUNION
you have nourished us in the mystery
of the body and blood of your Son:
By your grace keep us ever faithful to your word,
in the name of Jesus Christ our Lord. 16

Epiphany

The Epiphany
6 January

COLLECT ONE

O God,
who by the leading of a star
didst manifest thy only-begotten Son to the Gentiles;
Mercifully grant, that we, which know thee now by faith,
may after this life have the fruition of thy glorious Godhead;
through Jesus Christ our Lord.

COLLECT TWO

O God,
who by the leading of a star
manifested your only Son to the peoples of the earth:
Mercifully grant that we, who know you now by faith,
may at last behold your glory face to face;
through Jesus Christ our Lord. 1#

POST COMMUNION

Lord God,
the bright splendour whom the nations seek:
May we, who with the wise men
have been drawn by your light,
discern the glory of your presence in your incarnate Son;
who suffered, died, and was buried,
and who is alive and reigns with you and the Holy Spirit,
now and for ever. 8#

The First Sunday of Epiphany: The Baptism of our Lord

O Lord, COLLECT ONE
we beseech thee mercifully to receive
the prayers of thy people which call upon thee;
and grant that they may both perceive and know
what things they ought to do,
and also may have grace and power
faithfully to fulfill the same;
through Jesus Christ our Lord.

Eternal Father, COLLECT TWO
who at the baptism of Jesus
revealed him to be your Son,
anointing him with the Holy Spirit:
Grant to us, who are born of water and the Spirit,
that we may be faithful to our calling as your adopted children;
through Jesus Christ our Lord. 7#

Refreshed by these holy gifts, Lord God, POST COMMUNION
we seek your mercy:
that by listening faithfully to your only Son,
and being obedient to the prompting of the Spirit,
we may be your children in name and in truth;
through Jesus Christ our Lord. 20#

The Second Sunday of Epiphany

Almighty and everlasting God,
who dost govern all things in heaven and earth;
Mercifully hear the supplications of thy people,
and grant us thy peace all the days of our life;
through Jesus Christ our Lord.

COLLECT ONE

Almighty God,
in Christ you make all things new:
Transform the poverty of our nature
by the riches of your grace,
and in the renewal of our lives
make known your heavenly glory;
through Jesus Christ our Lord. 7

COLLECT TWO

God of glory,
you nourish us with bread from heaven.
Fill us with your Holy Spirit
that through us the light of your glory
may shine in all the world.
We ask this in the name of Jesus Christ our Lord. 16

POST COMMUNION

The Third Sunday of Epiphany

Almighty and everlasting God, COLLECT ONE
Mercifully look upon our infirmities,
and in all our dangers and necessities
stretch forth thy right hand to help and defend us;
through Jesus Christ our Lord.

Almighty God, COLLECT TWO
whose Son revealed in signs and miracles
the wonder of your saving presence:
Renew your people with your heavenly grace,
and in all our weakness
sustain us by your mighty power;
through Jesus Christ our Lord. 7

Almighty Father, POST COMMUNION
your Son our Saviour Jesus Christ is the light of the world.
May your people,
illumined by your word and sacraments,
shine with the radiance of his glory,
that he may be known, worshipped,
and obeyed to the ends of the earth;
for he is alive and reigns with you and the Holy Spirit,
one God, now and for ever. 16

The Fourth Sunday of Epiphany

O God,   COLLECT ONE
who knowest us to be set
in the midst of so many and great dangers,
that by reason of the frailty of our nature
we cannot always stand upright;
Grant to us such strength and protection,
as may support us in all dangers,
and carry us through all temptations;
through Jesus Christ our Lord.

Creator God,   COLLECT TWO
who in the beginning
commanded the light to shine out of darkness:
We pray that the light of the glorious gospel of Christ
may dispel the darkness of ignorance and unbelief,
shine into the hearts of all your people,
and reveal the knowledge of your glory
in the face of Jesus Christ our Lord. 8#

Generous Lord,   POST COMMUNION
in word and eucharist we have proclaimed
the mystery of your love.
Help us so to live out our days
that we may be signs of your wonders in the world;
through Jesus Christ our Saviour. 8

The Presentation of Christ in the Temple
2 February

May be observed on the Sunday between 28 January and 3 February.

Almighty and everliving God,   COLLECT ONE
we humbly beseech thy Majesty,
that, as thy only-begotten Son was this day
presented in the temple in substance of our flesh,
so we may be presented unto thee with pure and clean hearts,
by the same thy Son Jesus Christ our Lord.

Almighty and everliving God,   COLLECT TWO
clothed in majesty,
whose beloved Son was this day presented in the temple
in the substance of our mortal nature:
May we be presented to you with pure and clean hearts,
by your Son Jesus Christ our Lord. 1#

God, for whom we wait,   POST COMMUNION
you fulfilled the hopes of Simeon and Anna,
who lived to welcome the Messiah.
Complete in us your perfect will,
that in Christ we may see your salvation,
for he is Lord for ever and ever. 16#

Before Lent

The Fifth Sunday before Lent

Occurrence depends on date of Easter.

O Lord,   COLLECT ONE
we beseech thee to keep thy Church and household
continually in thy true religion;
that they who do lean only upon the hope of thy heavenly grace
may evermore be defended
by thy mighty power;
through Jesus Christ our Lord.

Almighty God,   COLLECT TWO
by whose grace alone we are accepted
and called to your service:
Strengthen us by your Holy Spirit
and make us worthy of our calling;
through Jesus Christ our Lord. 2

Merciful God,   POST COMMUNION
we thank you for inviting us to share
in the one bread and the one cup.
By your continuing grace
enable us to live as one family in Christ
and joyfully to seek to bring your salvation
to all who do not know you;
through Jesus Christ our Lord. 20#

The Fourth Sunday before Lent

Occurrence depends on date of Easter.

O Lord,   COLLECT ONE
we beseech thee favourably to hear the prayers of thy people;
that we, who are justly punished for our offences,
may be mercifully delivered by thy goodness,
for the glory of thy Name;
through Jesus Christ our Saviour,
who liveth and reigneth with thee and the Holy Spirit,
ever one God, world without end. Septuagesima

O God,   COLLECT TWO
you know us to be set
in the midst of so many and great dangers,
that by reason of the frailty of our nature
we cannot always stand upright:
Grant to us such strength and protection
as may support us in all dangers
and carry us through all temptations;
through Jesus Christ our Lord. 1#

God of tender care,   POST COMMUNION
in this eucharist we celebrate your love for us and for all people.
May we show your love in our lives
and know its fulfilment in your presence.
We ask this in the name of Jesus Christ our Lord. 16

The Third Sunday before Lent

Occurrence depends on date of Easter.

Lord,   COLLECT ONE
we beseech thee to keep thy household the Church
in continual godliness;
that through thy protection it may be free
from all adversities,
and devoutly given to serve thee in good works,
to the glory of thy name;
through Jesus Christ our Lord. Trinity 22

Almighty God,   COLLECT TWO
who alone can bring order
to the unruly wills and passions of sinful humanity:
Give your people grace
so to love what you command
and to desire what you promise;
that, among the many changes of the world,
our hearts may surely there be fixed
where true joys are to be found;
through Jesus Christ our Lord. 1#

Merciful Father,   POST COMMUNION
you gave Jesus Christ to be for us the bread of life,
that those who come to him should never hunger.
Draw us to our Lord in faith and love,
that we may eat and drink with him
at his table in the kingdom,
where he is alive and reigns with you and the Holy Spirit,
now and for ever. 2

The Second Sunday before Lent

Occurrence depends on date of Easter.

O Lord God,
who seest that we put not our trust
in any thing that we do;
Mercifully grant that by thy power
we may be defended against all adversity;
through Jesus Christ our Lord.   Sexagesima

Almighty God,
you have created the heavens and the earth
and made us in your own image:
Teach us to discern your hand in all your works
and your likeness in all your children;
through Jesus Christ our Lord,
who with you and the Holy Spirit
reigns supreme over all things, now and for ever.   2#

God our creator,
by your gift the tree of life was set at the heart
of the earthly paradise,
and the Bread of life at the heart of your Church.
May we who have been nourished at your table on earth
be transformed by the glory of the Saviour's Cross
and enjoy the delights of eternity;
through Jesus Christ our Lord.   II

The Sunday before Lent

O Lord,   COLLECT ONE
who hast taught us that all our doings without charity
are nothing worth;
Send thy Holy Spirit,
and pour into our hearts that most excellent gift of charity,
the very bond of peace and of all virtues,
without which whosoever liveth is counted dead before thee;
Grant this for thine only Son Jesus Christ's sake.   Quinquagesima

Almighty Father,   COLLECT TWO
whose Son was revealed in majesty
before he suffered death upon the cross:
Give us grace to perceive his glory,
that we may be strengthened to suffer with him
and be changed into his likeness, from glory to glory;
who is alive and reigns with you and the Holy Spirit,
one God, now and for ever. 7

or

O God, our Teacher and our Judge:
Enrich our hearts with the goodness of your wisdom
and renew us from within:
that all our actions, all our thoughts and all our words
may bear the fruit of your transforming grace;
through Jesus Christ our Lord. 20#

Holy God
we see your glory in the face of Jesus Christ.
May we who are partakers at his table
reflect his life in word and deed,
that all the world may know
his power to change and save.
This we ask through Jesus Christ our Lord.   16

or

Lord,
in this sacrament you have nourished us
with the spiritual food of the body and blood of your dear Son.
Not only with our lips
but with our lives may we truly confess his name,
and so enter the kingdom of heaven.
We ask this through Christ our Lord.   24

Lent

Ash Wednesday

Almighty and everlasting God, COLLECT ONE
who hatest nothing that thou hast made,
and dost forgive the sins of all them that are penitent;
Create and make in us new and contrite hearts,
that we worthily lamenting our sins,
and acknowledging our wretchedness,
may obtain of thee, the God of all mercy,
perfect remission and forgiveness;
through Jesus Christ our Lord.
This collect may be said after the Collect of the day until Easter Eve.

Almighty and everlasting God, COLLECT TWO
you hate nothing that you have made
and forgive the sins of all those who are penitent:
Create and make in us new and contrite hearts
that we, worthily lamenting our sins
and acknowledging our wretchedness,
may receive from you, the God of all mercy,
perfect remission and forgiveness;
through Jesus Christ our Lord. 1#

Almighty God, POST COMMUNION
you have given your only Son to be for us
both a sacrifice for sin and also an example of godly life:
Give us grace
that we may always most thankfully receive
these his inestimable gifts,
and also daily endeavour ourselves
to follow the blessed steps of his most holy life;
through Jesus Christ our Lord. 1#

The First Sunday in Lent

O Lord, COLLECT ONE
who for our sake didst fast forty days and forty nights;
Give us grace to use such abstinence,
that, our flesh being subdued to the Spirit,
we may ever obey thy godly motions
in righteousness,and true holiness,
to thy honour and glory,
who livest and reignest with the Father and the Holy Spirit,
one God, world without end.

Almighty God, COLLECT TWO
whose Son Jesus Christ fasted forty days in the wilderness,
and was tempted as we are, yet without sin:
Give us grace to discipline ourselves
in obedience to your Spirit;
and, as you know our weakness,
so may we know your power to save;
through Jesus Christ our Lord. 7

Lord God, POST COMMUNION
you renew us with the living bread from heaven.
Nourish our faith,
increase our hope,
strengthen our love,
and enable us to live by every word
that proceeds from out of your mouth;
through Jesus Christ our Lord. 17#

The Second Sunday in Lent

Almighty God,   COLLECT ONE
who seest that we have no power of ourselves to help ourselves;
Keep us both outwardly in our bodies,
and inwardly in our souls;
that we may be defended from all adversities
which may happen to the body,
and from all evil thoughts
which may assault and hurt the soul;
through Jesus Christ our Lord.

Almighty God,   COLLECT TWO
you show to those who are in error the light of your truth
that they may return to the way of righteousness:
Grant to all those who are admitted
into the fellowship of Christ's religion,
that they may reject those things
that are contrary to their profession,
and follow all such things
as are agreeable to the same;
through our Lord Jesus Christ.   1#

Creator of heaven and earth,   POST COMMUNION
we thank you for these holy mysteries
given us by our Lord Jesus Christ,
by which we receive your grace
and are assured of your love,
which is through him now and for ever.   24

The Third Sunday in Lent

We beseech thee, Almighty God,
COLLECT ONE
mercifully to look upon thy people;
that by thy great goodness
they may be governed and preserved evermore,
both in body and soul;
through Jesus Christ our Lord. 1926 Lent 5

Merciful Lord,
COLLECT TWO
Grant your people grace to withstand the temptations
of the world, the flesh and the devil
and with pure hearts and minds to follow you,
the only God;
through Jesus Christ our Lord. 1#

Lord our God,
POST COMMUNION
you feed us in this life with bread from heaven,
the pledge and foreshadowing of future glory.
Grant that the working of this sacrament within us
may bear fruit in our daily lives;
through Jesus Christ our Lord. 20

The Fourth Sunday in Lent
Mothering Sunday

Grant, we beseech thee, Almighty God, COLLECT ONE
that we, who for our evil deeds
do worthily deserve to be punished,
by the comfort of thy grace may mercifully be relieved;
through our Lord and Saviour Jesus Christ.

Lord God COLLECT TWO
whose blessed Son our Saviour
gave his back to the smiters
and did not hide his face from shame:
Give us grace to endure the sufferings of this present time
with sure confidence in the glory that shall be revealed;
through Jesus Christ our Lord. 1#

Or, for Mothering Sunday

God of compassion,
whose Son Jesus Christ, the child of Mary,
shared the life of a home in Nazareth,
and on the cross drew the whole human family to himself
Strengthen us in our daily living
that in joy and in sorrow
we may know the power of your presence
to bind together and to heal;
through Jesus Christ our Lord. 18

Father,
through your goodness
we are refreshed through your Son
in word and sacrament.
May our faith be so strengthened and guarded
that we may witness to your eternal love
by our words and in our lives.
Grant this for Jesus' sake, our Lord. 24

Or, for Mothering Sunday

Loving God,
as a mother feeds her children at the breast,
you feed us in this sacrament with spiritual food and drink.
Help us who have tasted your goodness
to grow in grace within the household of faith;
through Jesus Christ our Lord. 18#

Passiontide

The Fifth Sunday in Lent

We beseech thee, Almighty God, COLLECT ONE
look upon the hearty desires of thy humble servants,
and stretch forth the right hand of thy Majesty,
to be our defence against all our enemies;
through Jesus Christ our Lord.   1926 Lent 3

Most merciful God, COLLECT TWO
who by the death and resurrection of your Son Jesus Christ
delivered and saved the world:
Grant that by faith in him who suffered on the cross,
we may triumph in the power of his victory;
through Jesus Christ our Lord. 7

God of hope, POST COMMUNION
in this eucharist we have tasted
the promise of your heavenly banquet
and the richness of eternal life.
May we who bear witness to the death of your Son,
also proclaim the glory of his resurrection,
for he is Lord for ever and ever. 16

The Sixth Sunday in Lent: Palm Sunday

Almighty and everlasting God,
who, of thy tender love towards mankind,
hast sent thy Son, our Saviour Jesus Christ,
to take upon him our flesh,
and to suffer death upon the cross,
that all mankind should follow the example of his great humility;
Mercifully grant,
that we may both follow the example of his patience,
and also be made partakers of his resurrection;
through the same Jesus Christ our Lord.

Almighty and everlasting God,
who, in your tender love towards the human race,
sent your Son our Saviour Jesus Christ
to take upon him our flesh
and to suffer death upon the cross:
Grant that we may follow the example
of his patience and humility,
and also be made partakers of his resurrection;
through Jesus Christ our Lord. 1#

Lord Jesus Christ,
you humbled yourself in taking the form of a servant
and in obedience died on the cross for our salvation.
Give us the mind to follow you
and to proclaim you as Lord and King,
to the glory of God the Father. 2

Monday in Holy Week

Almighty and everlasting God, COLLECT ONE
who, of thy tender love towards mankind,
hast sent thy Son, our Saviour Jesus Christ,
to take upon him our flesh,
and to suffer death upon the cross,
that all mankind should follow the example of his great humility;
Mercifully grant,
that we may both follow the example of his patience,
and also be made partakers of his resurrection;
through the same Jesus Christ our Lord.

Almighty God, COLLECT TWO
whose most dear Son went not up to joy,
but first he suffered pain,
and entered not into glory before he was crucified:
Mercifully grant that we, walking in the way of his cross,
may find it none other than the way of life and peace;
through Jesus Christ our Lord. 2

Lord Jesus Christ, POST COMMUNION
you humbled yourself in taking the form of a servant
and in obedience died on the cross for our salvation.
Give us the mind to follow you
and to proclaim you as Lord and King,
to the glory of God the Father. 2

Tuesday in Holy Week

Almighty and everlasting God,   COLLECT ONE
who, of thy tender love towards mankind,
hast sent thy Son, our Saviour Jesus Christ,
to take upon him our flesh,
and to suffer death upon the cross,
that all mankind should follow the example of his great humility;
Mercifully grant,
that we may both follow the example of his patience,
and also be made partakers of his resurrection;
through the same Jesus Christ our Lord.

O God,   COLLECT TWO
who by the passion of your blessed Son made
an instrument of shameful death
to be for us the means of life:
Grant us so to glory in the cross of Christ,
that we may gladly suffer pain and loss
for the sake of your Son our Saviour Jesus Christ;
who lives and reigns with you and the Holy Spirit,
one God, now and for ever. 2

Lord Jesus Christ,   POST COMMUNION
you humbled yourself in taking the form of a servant
and in obedience died on the cross for our salvation.
give us the mind to follow you
and to proclaim you as Lord and King,
to the glory of God the Father. 2

Wednesday in Holy Week

Almighty and everlasting God,
who, of thy tender love towards mankind,
hast sent thy Son, our Saviour Jesus Christ,
to take upon him our flesh,
and to suffer death upon the cross,
that all mankind should follow the example of his great humility;
Mercifully grant,
that we may both follow the example of his patience,
and also be made partakers of his resurrection;
through the same Jesus Christ our Lord.

Lord God,   COLLECT TWO
whose blessed Son our Saviour
gave his back to the smiters,
and did not hide his face from shame:
Give us grace to endure the sufferings
of this present time,
with sure confidence in the glory that shall be revealed;
through Jesus Christ your Son our Lord.   2

Lord Jesus Christ,   POST COMMUNION
you humbled yourself in taking the form of a servant
and in obedience died on the cross for our salvation.
give us the mind to follow you
and to proclaim you as Lord and King,
to the glory of God the Father.   2

Maundy Thursday

O Lord,
who in a wonderful sacrament hast left us a memorial of thy passion;
Grant us so to reverence the sacred mysteries of thy body and blood
that we may perceive within ourselves
the fruits of thy redemption;
who livest and reignest with the Father and the Holy Spirit,
one God, now and for ever. Scottish Prayer Book 1929

or

Almighty and everlasting God,
who, of thy tender love towards mankind,
hast sent thy Son, our Saviour Jesus Christ,
to take upon him our flesh,
and to suffer death upon the cross,
that all mankind should follow the example of his great humility;
Mercifully grant,
that we may both follow the example of his patience,
and also be made partakers of his resurrection;
through the same Jesus Christ our Lord.

God our Father, COLLECT TWO
you have invited us to share in the supper
which your Son gave to his Church
to proclaim his death until he comes:
May he nourish us by his presence,
and unite us in his love;
who is alive and reigns with you and the Holy Spirit,
one God, now and for ever. 9

or

Almighty God,
at the Last Supper your Son Jesus Christ
washed the disciples' feet
and commanded them to love one another.
Give us humility and obedience to be servants of others
as he was the servant of all;
who gave up his life and died for us,
yet is alive and reigns with you and the Holy Spirit,
one God, now and for ever. 2#

Lord Jesus Christ,
in this wonderful sacrament
you have given us a memorial of your passion.
Grant us so to reverence the sacred mysteries
of your body and blood
that we may know within ourselves
the fruit of your redemption,
for you are alive and reign with the Father and the Holy Spirit,
one God, now and for ever. 2#

or

O God,
your Son Jesus Christ has left us this meal of bread and wine
in which we share his body and his blood.
May we who celebrate this sign of his great love
show in our lives the fruits of his redemption;
who is alive and reigns with you and the Holy Spirit,
one God, now and for ever. 16

Good Friday

Almighty God, COLLECTS ONE
we beseech thee graciously to behold this thy family,
for which our Lord Jesus Christ was contented to be betrayed,
and given up into the hands of wicked men,
and to suffer death upon the cross,
who now liveth and reigneth with thee
and the Holy Spirit, ever one God, world without end.

Almighty and everlasting God,
by whose Spirit the whole body of the Church
is governed and sanctified;
Receive our supplications and prayers,
which we offer before thee for all estates of men
in thy holy Church,
that every member of the same,
in his vocation and ministry,
may truly and godly serve thee;
through our Lord and Saviour Jesus Christ.

Almighty Father, COLLECT TWO
Look with mercy on this your family
for which our Lord Jesus Christ
was content to be betrayed
and given up into the hands of sinners
and to suffer death upon the cross;
who is alive and glorified with you and the Holy Spirit,
one God, now and for ever. ɪ#

No Post Communion is provided for Good Friday.

Easter Eve

Grant, O Lord,
that as we are baptized into the death
of thy blessed Son our Saviour Jesus Christ,
so by continual mortifying our corrupt affections
we may be buried with him;
and that, through the grave, and gate of death,
we may pass to our joyful resurrection;
for his merits, who died, and was buried,
and rose again for us,
thy Son Jesus Christ our Lord.

COLLECT ONE

Grant, Lord,
that we who are baptized into the death
of your Son our Saviour Jesus Christ
may continually put to death our evil desires
and be buried with him;
and that through the grave and gate of death
we may pass to our joyful resurrection;
through his merits, who died and was buried
and rose again for us,
your Son Jesus Christ our Lord.   1#

COLLECT TWO

No Post Communion is provided for Easter Eve.

Eastertide

The First Sunday of Easter: Easter Day

Almighty God,   COLLECT ONE
who through thine only-begotten Son Jesus Christ
hast overcome death,
and opened unto us the gate of everlasting life;
We humbly beseech thee,
that, as by thy special grace preventing us
thou dost put into our minds good desires,
so by thy continual help we may bring the same to good effect;
through Jesus Christ our Lord,
who liveth and reigneth with thee and the Holy Spirit,
ever one God, world without end.

*If there are two celebrations of the Holy Communion this collect may be used
at the first.*

O God,
who for our redemption didst give thine only-begotten Son
to the death of the cross,
and by his glorious resurrection
hast delivered us from the power of our enemy;
Grant us so to die daily from sin,
that we may evermore live with him in the joy of his resurrection;
through the same Christ our Lord.

Almighty God,
through your only-begotten Son Jesus Christ
you have overcome death
and opened to us the gate of everlasting life:
Grant that, as by your grace going before us
you put into our minds good desires,
so by your continual help we may bring them to good effect;
through Jesus Christ our risen Lord
who is alive and reigns with you and the Holy Spirit,
one God, now and for ever. 1#

Living God,
for our redemption you gave your only-begotten Son
to the death of the cross,
and by his glorious resurrection
you have delivered us from the power of our enemy.
Grant us so to die daily unto sin,
that we may evermore live with him in the joy of his risen life;
through Jesus Christ our Lord. 4#

The Second Sunday of Easter

COLLECT ONE

Almighty Father,
who hast given thine only Son to die for our sins,
and to rise again for our justification;
Grant us so to put away the leaven
of malice and wickedness,
that we may alway serve thee in pureness of living and truth;
through the merits of the same thy Son
Jesus Christ our Lord.

COLLECT TWO

Almighty Father,
you have given your only Son to die for our sins
and to rise again for our justification:
Grant us so to put away the leaven
of malice and wickedness
that we may always serve you in pureness of living and truth;
through the merits of your Son
Jesus Christ our Lord. 1#

POST COMMUNION

Lord God our Father,
through our Saviour Jesus Christ
you have assured your children of eternal life
and in baptism have made us one with him.
Deliver us from the death of sin
and raise us to new life in your love,
in the fellowship of the Holy Spirit,
by the grace of our Lord Jesus Christ. 7

The Third Sunday of Easter

Almighty God,   COLLECT ONE
who hast given thine only Son
to be unto us both a sacrifice for sin,
and also an ensample of godly life;
Give us grace that we may always
most thankfully receive that his inestimable benefit,
and also daily endeavour ourselves
to follow the blessed steps of his most holy life;
through the same Jesus Christ our Lord.

Almighty Father,   COLLECT TWO
who in your great mercy gladdened the disciples
with the sight of the risen Lord:
Give us such knowledge of his presence with us,
that we may be strengthened
and sustained by his risen life
and serve you continually in righteousness and truth;
through Jesus Christ our Lord. 7

Living God,   POST COMMUNION
your Son made himself known to his disciples
in the breaking of bread.
Open the eyes of our faith,
that we may see him in all his redeeming work;
who is alive and reigns with you and the Holy Spirit,
one God, now and for ever. 16

The Fourth Sunday of Easter

Almighty God, COLLECT ONE
who shewest to them that be in error
the light of thy truth,
to the intent that they may return
into the way of righteousness;
Grant unto all them that are admitted
into the fellowship of Christ's Religion,
that they may eschew those things
that are contrary to their profession,
and follow all such things as are agreeable to the same;
through our Lord Jesus Christ.

Almighty God, COLLECT TWO
whose Son Jesus Christ is the resurrection and the life:
Raise us, who trust in him,
from the death of sin to the life of righteousness,
that we may seek those things which are above,
where he reigns with you and the Holy Spirit,
one God, now and for ever. 7

Merciful Father, POST COMMUNION
you gave your Son Jesus Christ to be the good shepherd,
and in his love for us to lay down his life and rise again.
Keep us always under his protection,
and give us grace to follow in his steps;
through Jesus Christ our Lord. 2

This may be used as Collect Two in year A.

The Fifth Sunday of Easter

O Almighty God, COLLECT ONE
who alone canst order the unruly wills and affections
of sinful men;
Grant unto thy people,
that they may love the thing which thou commandest,
and desire that which thou dost promise;
that so, among the sundry and manifold changes of the world,
our hearts may surely there be fixed,
where true joys are to be found;
through Jesus Christ our Lord.

Lord of all life and power, COLLECT TWO
who through the mighty resurrection of your Son
overcame the old order of sin and death
to make all things new in him:
Grant that we, being dead to sin
and alive to you in Jesus Christ,
may reign with him in glory;
to whom with you and the Holy Spirit
be praise and honour, glory and might,
now and in all eternity. 7

Eternal God, POST COMMUNION
in word and sacrament
we proclaim your truth in Jesus Christ and share his life.
In his strength may we ever walk in his way,
who is alive and reigns with you and the Holy Spirit,
one God, now and for ever. 24#

The Sixth Sunday of Easter: Rogation Sunday

O Lord,   COLLECT ONE
from whom all good things do come;
Grant to us thy humble servants,
that by thy holy inspiration
we may think those things that be good,
and by thy merciful guiding may perform the same;
through our Lord Jesus Christ.

God our redeemer,   COLLECT TWO
you have delivered us from the power of darkness
and brought us into the kingdom of your Son:
Grant, that as by his death he has recalled us to life,
so by his continual presence in us he may raise us to eternal joy;
through Jesus Christ our Lord. 9#

God our Father,   POST COMMUNION
whose Son Jesus Christ gives the water of eternal life:
May we also thirst for you.
the spring of life and source of goodness,
through him who is alive and reigns with you
and the Holy Spirit,
one God, now and for ever. 16

The Ascension Day

Grant, we beseech thee, Almighty God, COLLECT ONE
that like as we do believe thy only-begotten Son
our Lord Jesus Christ
to have ascended into the heavens;
So we may also in heart and mind thither ascend,
and with him continually dwell,
who liveth and reigneth with thee and the Holy Spirit,
one God, world without end.

Grant, we pray, Almighty God, COLLECT TWO
that as we believe your only-begotten Son our Lord Jesus Christ
to have ascended into the heavens;
so we in heart and mind may also ascend
and with him continually dwell;
who is alive and reigns with you and the Holy Spirit,
one God, now and for ever. 1#

God our Father, POST COMMUNION
you have raised our humanity in Christ
and feed us with the bread of heaven.
Mercifully grant that, nourished with such spiritual blessings,
we may set our hearts in the heavenly places;
where he now lives and reigns for ever. 18#

The Seventh Sunday of Easter:
Sunday after Ascension Day

O God the King of glory,
who hast exalted thine only Son Jesus Christ
with great triumph unto thy kingdom in heaven;
We beseech thee, leave us not comfortless;
but send to us thine Holy Spirit to comfort us,
and exalt us unto the same place
whither our Saviour Christ is gone before,
who liveth and reigneth with thee and the Holy Spirit,
one God, world without end.

O God the King of Glory,
you have exalted your only Son Jesus Christ
with great triumph to your kingdom in heaven:
Mercifully give us faith to know
that, as he promised,
he abides with us on earth to the end of time;
who is alive and reigns with you and the Holy Spirit,
one God, now and for ever. 16#

Eternal Giver of love and power,
your Son Jesus Christ has sent us into all the world
to preach the gospel of his kingdom.
Confirm us in this mission,
and help us to live the good news we proclaim;
through Jesus Christ our Lord. 16

Day of Pentecost: Whitsunday

God, COLLECT ONE
who as at this time didst teach the hearts of thy faithful people,
by the sending to them the light of thy Holy Spirit;
Grant us by the same Spirit
to have a right judgement in all things,
and evermore to rejoice in his holy comfort;
through the merits of Christ Jesus our Saviour,
who liveth and reigneth with thee,
in the unity of the same Spirit, one God, world without end.

Almighty God, COLLECT TWO
who on the day of Pentecost
sent your Holy Spirit to the apostles
with the wind from heaven and in tongues of flame,
filling them with joy and boldness to preach the gospel:
By the power of the same Spirit
strengthen us to witness to your truth
and to draw everyone to the fire of your love;
through Jesus Christ our Lord. 2#

Faithful God, POST COMMUNION
who fulfilled the promises of Easter
by sending us your Holy Spirit
and opening to every race and nation the way of life eternal:
Open our lips by your Spirit,
that every tongue may tell of your glory;
through Jesus Christ our Lord. 16#

After Pentecost to before Advent

Weekdays after the Day of Pentecost

O Lord,   COLLECT ONE
from whom all good things do come;
Grant to us thy humble servants,
that by thy holy inspiration
we may think those things that be good,
and by thy merciful guiding may perform the same;
through our Lord Jesus Christ. 1926 Easter 5

O Lord, from whom all good things come: COLLECT TWO
Grant to us your humble servants,
that, by your holy inspiration
we may think those things that be good,
and by your merciful guiding may perform the same;
through our Lord Jesus Christ. 1#

Gracious God, lover of all,   POST COMMUNION
in this sacrament
we are one family in Christ your Son,
one in the sharing of his body and blood,
and one in the communion of his Spirit.
Help us to grow in love for one another
and come to the full maturity of the Body of Christ.
We make our prayer through your Son our Saviour. 16

Trinity Sunday

Almighty and everlasting God,   COLLECT ONE
who hast given unto us thy servants grace
by the confession of a true faith
to acknowledge the glory of the eternal Trinity,
and in the power of the Divine Majesty to worship the Unity;
We beseech thee,
that thou wouldest keep us steadfast in this faith,
and evermore defend us from all adversities,
who livest and reignest, one God, world without end.

Almighty and everlasting God,   COLLECT TWO
you have given us your servants grace,
by the confession of a true faith,
to acknowledge the glory of the eternal Trinity
and in the power of the divine majesty to worship the Unity:
Keep us steadfast in this faith,
that we may evermore be defended from all adversities;
for you live and reign, one God, for ever and ever. 1#

Almighty God,   POST COMMUNION
may we who have received this holy communion,
worship you with lips and lives
proclaiming your majesty
and finally see you in your eternal glory:
Holy and Eternal Trinity,
one God, now and for ever. 24

The First Sunday after Trinity

O God, COLLECT ONE

the strength of all them that put their trust in thee;
Mercifully accept our prayers;
and because through the weakness of our mortal nature
we can do no good thing without thee,
grant us the help of thy grace,
that in keeping of thy commandments
we may please thee both in will and deed;
through Jesus Christ our Lord.

God, COLLECT TWO

the strength of all those who put their trust in you:
Mercifully accept our prayers
and, because through the weakness of our mortal nature
we can do no good thing without you,
grant us the help of your grace,
that in the keeping of your commandments
we may please you, both in will and deed;
through Jesus Christ our Lord. 1#

Eternal Father, POST COMMUNION

we thank you for nourishing us
with these heavenly gifts.
May our communion strengthen us in faith,
build us up in hope,
and make us grow in love;
for the sake of Jesus Christ our Lord. 8

The Second Sunday after Trinity

O Lord, COLLECT ONE
who never failest to help and govern them
whom thou dost bring up in thy steadfast fear and love;
Keep us, we beseech thee,
under the protection of thy good providence,
and make us to have a perpetual fear and love of thy holy Name;
through Jesus Christ our Lord.

Lord, you have taught us COLLECT TWO
that all our doings without love are nothing worth:
Send your Holy Spirit
and pour into our hearts that most excellent gift of love,
the true bond of peace and of all virtues,
without which whoever lives is counted dead before you.
Grant this for your only Son Jesus Christ's sake. 1#

Loving Father, POST COMMUNION
we thank you for feeding us at the supper of your Son.
Sustain us with your Spirit,
that we may serve you here on earth
until our joy is complete in heaven,
and we share in the eternal banquet
with Jesus Christ our Lord. 8

The Third Sunday after Trinity

O Lord,   COLLECT ONE
we beseech thee mercifully to hear us;
and grant that we, to whom thou hast given
an hearty desire to pray,
may by thy mighty aid be defended and comforted
in all dangers and adversities;
through Jesus Christ our Lord.

Almighty God,   COLLECT TWO
you have broken the tyranny of sin
and have sent the Spirit of your Son into our hearts
whereby we call you Father:
Give us grace to dedicate our freedom to your service,
that we and all creation may be brought
to the glorious liberty of the children of God;
through Jesus Christ our Lord. 7

O God,   POST COMMUNION
whose beauty is beyond our imagining
and whose power we cannot comprehend:
Give us a glimpse of your glory on earth
but shield us from knowing more than we can bear
until we may look upon you without fear;
through Jesus Christ our Saviour. 3#

The Fourth Sunday after Trinity

O God, the protector of all that trust in thee,
without whom nothing is strong, nothing is holy;
Increase and multiply upon us thy mercy;
that, thou being our ruler and guide,
we may so pass through things temporal,
that we finally lose not the things eternal:
Grant this, O heavenly Father,
for Jesus Christ's sake our Lord.

COLLECT ONE

O God, the protector of all who trust in you,
without whom nothing is strong, nothing is holy:
Increase and multiply upon us your mercy;
that with you as our ruler and guide,
we may so pass through things temporal
that we finally lose not the things eternal:
Grant this, heavenly Father,
for Jesus Christ's sake, our Lord. 1#

COLLECT TWO

Eternal God,
comfort of the afflicted and healer of the broken,
you have fed us at the table of life and hope.
Teach us the ways of gentleness and peace,
that all the world may acknowledge
the kingdom of your Son Jesus Christ our Lord. 16

POST COMMUNION

The Fifth Sunday after Trinity

Grant, O Lord, we beseech thee, COLLECT ONE
that the course of this world
may be so peaceably ordered by thy governance,
that thy Church may joyfully serve thee
in all godly quietness;
through Jesus Christ our Lord.

Almighty and everlasting God, COLLECT TWO
by whose Spirit the whole body of the Church
is governed and sanctified:
Hear our prayer which we offer for all your faithful people,
that in their vocation and ministry
they may serve you in holiness and truth
to the glory of your name;
through our Lord and Saviour Jesus Christ. 1#

Holy and blessed God, POST COMMUNION
as you give us the body and blood of your Son,
guide us with your Holy Spirit,
that we may honour you not only with our lips
but also with our lives;
through Jesus Christ our Lord. 16

The Sixth Sunday after Trinity

O God,
who hast prepared for them that love thee
such good things as pass man's understanding;
Pour into our hearts such love toward thee,
that we, loving thee above all things,
may obtain thy promises,
which exceed all that we can desire:;
through Jesus Christ our Lord.

COLLECT ONE

Merciful God,
you have prepared for those who love you
such good things as pass our understanding:
Pour into our hearts such love toward you
that we, loving you above all things,
may obtain your promises,
which exceed all that we can desire;
through Jesus Christ our Lord. 1#

COLLECT TWO

God of our pilgrimage.
you have led us to the living water.
Refresh and sustain us
as we go forward on our journey,
in the name of Jesus Christ our Lord. 16

POST COMMUNION

The Seventh Sunday after Trinity

Lord of all power and might,
who art the author and giver of all good things;
Graft in our hearts the love of thy Name,
increase in us true religion,
nourish us with all goodness,
and of thy great mercy keep us in the same;
through Jesus Christ our Lord.

COLLECT ONE

Lord of all power and might,
the author and giver of all good things:
Graft in our hearts the love of your name,
increase in us true religion,
nourish us with all goodness,
and of your great mercy keep us in the same;
through Jesus Christ our Lord. 1#

COLLECT TWO

Lord God,
whose Son is the true vine and the source of life,
ever giving himself that the world may live:
May we so receive within ourselves
the power of his death and passion
that, in his saving cup,
we may share his glory and be made perfect in his love;
for he is alive and reigns with you and the Holy Spirit,
now and for ever. 8

POST COMMUNION

The Eighth Sunday after Trinity

O God, COLLECT ONE
whose never-failing providence ordereth all things
both in heaven and earth;
We humbly beseech thee to put away from us
all hurtful things,
and to give us those things which be profitable for us;
through Jesus Christ our Lord.

Blessed are you, O Lord, COLLECT TWO
and blessed are those who observe and keep your law:
Help us to seek you with our whole heart,
to delight in your commandments
and to walk in the glorious liberty
given us by your Son, Jesus Christ.   15

Strengthen for service, Lord, POST COMMUNION
the hands that holy things have taken;
may the ears which have heard your word
be deaf to clamour and dispute;
may the tongues which have sung your praise
be free from deceit;
may the eyes which have seen the tokens of your love
shine with the light of hope;
and may the bodies which have been fed with your body
be refreshed with the fulness of your life;
glory to you for ever.   18

The Ninth Sunday after Trinity

Grant to us, Lord, we beseech thee,
the spirit to think and do always
such things as be rightful;
that we, who cannot do any thing
that is good without thee,
may by thee be enabled to live according to thy will;
through Jesus Christ our Lord.

Almighty God,
who sent your Holy Spirit
to be the life and light of your Church:
Open our hearts to the riches of his grace,
that we may bring forth the fruit of the Spirit
in love and joy and peace;
through Jesus Christ our Lord. 2

Holy Father,
who gathered us here around the table of your Son
to share this meal with the whole household of God:
In that new world where you reveal the fulness of your peace,
gather people of every race and language
to share in the eternal banquet
of Jesus Christ our Lord. 19#

The Tenth Sunday after Trinity

Let thy merciful ears, O Lord,
be open to the prayers of thy humble servants;
and that they may obtain their petitions,
make them to ask such things as shall please thee;
through Jesus Christ our Lord.

COLLECT ONE

Let your merciful ears, O Lord,
be open to the prayers of your humble servants;
and that they may obtain their petitions,
make them to ask such things as shall please you;
through Jesus Christ our Lord. 1#

COLLECT TWO

O God,
as we are strengthened by these holy mysteries,
so may our lives be a continual offering,
holy and acceptable in your sight;
through Jesus Christ our Lord. 16

POST COMMUNION

The Eleventh Sunday after Trinity

O God, COLLECT ONE
who declarest thy almighty power
most chiefly in shewing mercy and pity;
Mercifully grant unto us such a measure of thy grace,
that we, running the way of thy commandments,
may obtain thy gracious promises,
and be made partakers of thy heavenly treasure;
through Jesus Christ our Lord.

O God, COLLECT TWO
you declare your almighty power
most chiefly in showing mercy and pity:
Mercifully grant to us such a measure of your grace,
that we, running the way of your commandments,
may receive your gracious promises,
and be made partakers of your heavenly treasure;
through Jesus Christ our Lord. 1#

Lord of all mercy, POST COMMUNION
we your faithful people have celebrated
the memorial of that single sacrifice
which takes away our sins and brings pardon and peace.
By our communion
keep us firm on the foundation of the gospel
and preserve us from all sin;
through Jesus Christ our Lord. 10#

The Twelfth Sunday after Trinity

Almighty and everlasting God,
who art always more ready to hear than we to pray,
and art wont to give more than either we desire, or deserve;
Pour down upon us the abundance of thy mercy;
forgiving us those things whereof our conscience is afraid,
and giving us those good things
which we are not worthy to ask,
but through the merits and mediation
of Jesus Christ, thy Son, our Lord.

Almighty and everlasting God, COLLECT TWO
you are always more ready to hear than we to pray
and to give more than either we desire, or deserve:
Pour down upon us the abundance of your mercy,
forgiving us those things of which our conscience is afraid,
and giving us those good things
which we are not worthy to ask
save through the merits and mediation
of Jesus Christ your Son our Lord. 1#

God of compassion, POST COMMUNION
in this eucharist we know again your forgiveness
and the healing power of your love.
Grant that we who are made whole in Christ
may bring that forgiveness and healing to this broken world,
in the name of Jesus Christ our Lord. 16#

The Thirteenth Sunday after Trinity

Almighty and merciful God,   COLLECT ONE
of whose only gift it cometh
that thy faithful people do unto thee true and laudable service;
Grant, we beseech thee,
that we may so faithfully serve thee in this life,
that we fail not finally to attain thy heavenly promises;
through the merits of Jesus Christ our Lord.

Almighty God,   COLLECT TWO
who called your Church to bear witness
that you were in Christ reconciling the world to yourself:
Help us to proclaim the good news of your love,
that all who hear it may be drawn to you;
through him who was lifted up on the cross,
and reigns with you and the Holy Spirit,
one God, now and for ever. 7#

God our creator,   POST COMMUNION
you feed your children with the true manna,
the living bread from heaven.
Let this holy food sustain us through our earthly pilgrimage
until we come to that place
where hunger and thirst are no more;
through Jesus Christ our Lord. 12

The Fourteenth Sunday after Trinity

Almighty and everlasting God,
Give unto us the increase of faith, hope, and charity;
and, that we may obtain that which thou dost promise,
make us to love that which thou dost command;
through Jesus Christ our Lord.

COLLECT ONE

Almighty God,
whose only Son has opened for us
a new and living way into your presence:
Give us pure hearts and steadfast wills
to worship you in spirit and in truth,
through Jesus Christ our Lord   7

COLLECT TWO

Lord God,
the source of truth and love:
Keep us faithful to the apostles' teaching and fellowship,
united in prayer and the breaking of bread,
and one in joy and simplicity of heart,
in Jesus Christ our Lord.   13

POST COMMUNION

The Fifteenth Sunday after Trinity

Keep, we beseech thee, COLLECT ONE
O Lord, thy Church with thy perpetual mercy;
and, because the frailty of man without thee cannot but fall,
keep us ever by thy help from all things hurtful,
and lead us to all things profitable to our salvation;
through Jesus Christ our Lord.

God, COLLECT TWO
who in generous mercy sent the Holy Spirit
upon your Church in the burning fire of your love:
Grant that your people may be fervent
in the fellowship of the gospel;
that, always abiding in you,
they may be found steadfast in faith and active in service;
through Jesus Christ our Lord. 12#

Eternal God, POST COMMUNION
we have received these tokens of your promise.
May we who have been nourished with holy things
live as faithful heirs of your promised kingdom.
We ask this in the name of Jesus Christ our Lord. 16

The Sixteenth Sunday after Trinity

O Lord, we beseech thee,
let thy continual pity cleanse and defend thy Church;
and, because it cannot continue in safety
without thy succour,
preserve it evermore by thy help and goodness;
through Jesus Christ our Lord.

O Lord,
Hear the prayers of your people who call upon you;
and grant that they may both perceive and know
what things they ought to do,
and also may have grace and power
faithfully to fulfil them;
through Jesus Christ our Lord. 1#

God of mercy,
through our sharing in this holy sacrament
you make us one body in Christ.
Fashion us in his likeness here on earth,
that we may share his glorious company in heaven,
where he lives and reigns now and for ever. 20#

The Seventeenth Sunday after Trinity

Lord, we pray thee COLLECT ONE
that thy grace may always prevent and follow us,
and make us continually to be given to all good works;
through Jesus Christ our Lord.

Almighty God, COLLECT TWO
you have made us for yourself,
and our hearts are restless till they find their rest in you:
Teach us to offer ourselves to your service,
that here we may have your peace,
and in the world to come may see you face to face;
through Jesus Christ our Lord. 2

God our guide. POST COMMUNION
you feed us with bread from heaven
as you fed your people Israel.
May we who have been inwardly nourished
be ready to follow you
all the days of our pilgrimage on earth,
until we come to your kingdom in heaven.
This we ask in the name of Jesus Christ our Lord. 16#

The Eighteenth Sunday after Trinity

Lord, we beseech thee, COLLECT ONE
Grant thy people grace to withstand the temptations
of the world, the flesh, and the devil,
and with pure hearts and minds to follow thee
the only God;
through Jesus Christ our Lord.

Almighty and everlasting God: COLLECT TWO
Increase in us your gift of faith
that, forsaking what lies behind,
we may run the way of your commandments
and win the crown of everlasting joy;
through Jesus Christ our Lord. 7

All praise and thanks, O Christ, POST COMMUNION
for this sacred banquet,
in which by faith we receive you,
the memory of your passion is renewed,
our lives are filled with grace,
and a pledge of future glory given,
to feast at that table where you reign
with all your saints for ever. 21#

The Nineteenth Sunday after Trinity

The Fifth Sunday before Advent takes precedence.

O God,   COLLECT ONE
forasmuch as without thee
we are not able to please thee;
Mercifully grant, that thy Holy Spirit
may in all things direct and rule our hearts;
through Jesus Christ our Lord.

O God,   COLLECT TWO
without you we are not able to please you;
Mercifully grant that your Holy Spirit
may in all things direct and rule our hearts;
through Jesus Christ our Lord. 1#

Holy and blessed God,   POST COMMUNION
you feed us with the body and blood of your Son
and fill us with your Holy Spirit.
May we honour you,
not only with our lips but in lives dedicated
to the service of Jesus Christ our Lord. 19

The Twentieth Sunday after Trinity

The Fifth Sunday before Advent takes precedence.

O Almighty and most merciful God, COLLECT ONE
of thy bountiful goodness keep us, we beseech thee,
from all things that may hurt us;
that we, being ready both in body and soul,
may cheerfully accomplish those things
that thou wouldest have done;
through Jesus Christ our Lord.

Almighty God, COLLECT TWO
whose Holy Spirit equips your Church with a rich variety of gifts:
Grant us so to use them that, living the gospel of Christ
and eager to do your will,
we may share with the whole creation
in the joys of eternal life;
through Jesus Christ our Lord. 7#

God our Father, POST COMMUNION
whose Son, the light unfailing,
has come from heaven to deliver the world
from the darkness of ignorance:
Let these holy mysteries open the eyes of our understanding
that we may know the way of life,
and walk in it without stumbling;
through Jesus Christ our Lord. 12

The Twenty-first Sunday after Trinity

The Fifth Sunday before Advent takes precedence.

Grant, we beseech thee, merciful Lord,
to thy faithful people pardon and peace;
that they may be cleansed from all their sins,
and serve thee with a quiet mind;
through Jesus Christ our Lord.

Merciful Lord,
Grant to your faithful people pardon and peace,
that we may be cleansed from all our sins
and serve you with a quiet mind;
through Jesus Christ our Lord. 1#

Father of light,
in whom is no change or shadow of turning,
you give us every good and perfect gift
and have brought us to birth by your word of truth.
May we be a living sign of that kingdom,
where your whole creation will be made perfect
in Jesus Christ our Lord. 14

The Fifth Sunday before Advent

Blessed Lord, COLLECT ONE
who hast caused all holy Scriptures to be written for our learning;
Grant that we may in such wise hear them,
read, mark, learn and inwardly digest them,
that by patience, and comfort of thy holy Word,
we may embrace, and ever hold fast
the blessed hope of everlasting life,
which thou hast given us
in our Saviour Jesus Christ. 1926 Advent 2

Blessed Lord, COLLECT TWO
who caused all holy Scriptures to be written for our learning:
Help us to hear them,
to read, mark, learn and inwardly digest them
that, through patience, and the comfort of your holy word,
we may embrace and for ever hold fast
the blessed hope of everlasting life,
which you have given us in our Saviour Jesus Christ. 1#

God of all grace, POST COMMUNION
your Son Jesus Christ fed the hungry
with the bread of his life and the word of his kingdom.
Renew your people with your heavenly grace,
and in all our weakness
sustain us by your true and living bread,
who is alive and reigns with you and the Holy Spirit,
one God, now and for ever. 16#

All Saints' Day
1 November

May be observed on the nearest Sunday

O almighty God,   COLLECT ONE
who hast knit together thine elect
in one communion and fellowship,
in the mystical body of thy Son Christ our Lord;
Grant us so to follow thy blessed Saints
in all virtuous and godly living,
that we may come to those unspeakable joys,
which thou hast prepared for them that unfeignedly love thee;
through Jesus Christ our Lord.

Almighty God,   COLLECT TWO
you have knit together your elect
in one communion and fellowship
in the mystical body of your Son Christ our Lord:
Grant us grace so to follow your blessed saints
in all virtuous and godly living
that we may come to those inexpressible joys
that you have prepared for those who truly love you;
through Jesus Christ our Lord. 1#

God, the source of all holiness   POST COMMUNION
and giver of all good things:
May we, who have shared at this table
as strangers and pilgrims here on earth,
be welcomed with all your saints
to the heavenly feast on the day of your kingdom;
through Jesus Christ our Lord. 8

The Fourth Sunday before Advent

O God, our refuge and strength,   Collect One
who art the author of all godliness;
Be ready, we beseech thee, to hear
the devout prayers of thy Church;
and grant that those things which we ask faithfully
we may obtain effectually;
through Jesus Christ our Lord.

Almighty and eternal God,   Collect Two
you have kindled the flame of love in the hearts of the saints:
Grant to us the same faith and power of love,
that, as we rejoice in their triumphs,
we may be sustained by their example and fellowship;
through Jesus Christ our Lord. 8

Lord of heaven,   Post Communion
in this eucharist you have brought us near
to an innumerable company of angels
and to the spirits of the saints made perfect.
As in this food of our earthly pilgrimage
we have shared their fellowship,
so may we come to share their joy in heaven;
through Jesus Christ our Lord. 12

The Third Sunday before Advent

O Lord, we beseech thee,
absolve thy people from their offences;
that through thy bountiful goodness
we may all be delivered from the bonds of those sins,
which by our frailty we have committed;
Grant this, O heavenly Father, for Jesus Christ's sake,
our blessed Lord and Saviour.

COLLECT ONE

Almighty Father,
whose will is to restore all things
in your beloved Son, the king of all:
Govern the hearts and minds of those in authority,
and bring the families of the nations,
divided and torn apart by the ravages of sin,
to be subject to his just and gentle rule;
who is alive and reigns with you and the Holy Spirit,
one God, now and for ever. 7

COLLECT TWO

God of peace,
whose Son Jesus Christ proclaimed the kingdom
and restored the broken to wholeness of life:
Look with compassion on the anguish of the world,
and by your healing power
make whole both people and nations;
through our Lord and Saviour Jesus Christ. 7

POST COMMUNION

The Second Sunday before Advent

O God, COLLECT ONE
whose blessed Son was manifested
that he might destroy the works of the devil,
and make us the sons of God, and heirs of eternal life;
Grant us, we beseech thee, that, having this hope,
we may purify ourselves, even as he is pure;
that, when he shall appear again with power and great glory,
we may be made like unto him
in his eternal and glorious kingdom;
where with thee, O Father, and thee, O Holy Spirit,
he liveth and reigneth, ever one God, world without end.

Heavenly Father, COLLECT TWO
whose blessed Son was revealed to destroy the works of the devil
and make us the children of God
and heirs of eternal life:
Grant that we, having this hope,
may purify ourselves even as he is pure;
that when he shall appear in power and great glory
we may be made like him
in his eternal and glorious kingdom;
where he is alive and reigns with you and the Holy Spirit,
one God, now and for ever. 1#

Gracious Lord, POST COMMUNION
in this holy sacrament you give substance to our hope.
Bring us at the last to that pure life for which we long,
through Jesus Christ our Saviour. 8#

The Sunday before Advent:
The Kingship of Christ

Stir up, we beseech thee, O Lord, COLLECT ONE
the wills of thy faithful people;
that they, plenteously bringing forth the fruit of good works,
may of thee be plenteously rewarded;
through Jesus Christ our Lord.

Eternal Father, COLLECT TWO
whose Son Jesus Christ ascended to the throne of heaven
that he might rule over all things as Lord and King:
Keep the Church in the unity of the Spirit
and in the bond of peace,
and bring the whole created order to worship at his feet,
who is alive and reigns with you and the Holy Spirit,
one God, now and for ever. 2#

Stir up, O Lord, POST COMMUNION
the wills of your faithful people;
that plenteously bearing the fruit of good works
they may by you be plenteously rewarded;
through Jesus Christ our Lord. 1#

Weekdays of the week before Advent

Stir up, we beseech thee, O Lord, COLLECT ONE
the wills of thy faithful people;
that they, plenteously bringing forth the fruit of good works,
may of thee be plenteously rewarded;
through Jesus Christ our Lord.

Stir up, O Lord, COLLECT TWO
the wills of your faithful people;
that plenteously bearing the fruit of good works
they may by you be plenteously rewarded;
through Jesus Christ our Lord. 1#

All powerful God, POST COMMUNION
by giving us a share in these divine mysteries
you gladden our hearts.
Remain with us now
and let us never be separated from you.
Grant this through Jesus Christ our Lord. 20#

Festivals

Naming and Circumcision of Jesus 1 January

Almighty God, COLLECT ONE
who madest thy blessed Son to be circumcised,
and obedient to the law for man;
Grant us the true circumcision of the Spirit;
that, our hearts and all our members being mortified
from all worldly and carnal lusts,
we may in all things obey thy holy will;
through the same thy Son Jesus Christ our Lord..

Almighty God, COLLECT TWO
whose blessed Son was circumcised
in obedience to the law for our sake
and given the Name that declares your saving love:
Give us grace faithfully to bear his Name,
to worship him in the freedom of the Spirit,
and to proclaim him as the Saviour of the world;
who is alive and reigns with you and the Holy Spirit,
one God, now and for ever. 1#

Eternal God, POST COMMUNION
whose incarnate Son was given the name of Saviour:
Grant that we who have shared in this sacrament of our salvation
may live out our years
in the power of the name of Jesus Christ our Lord. 1#

The Conversion of Saint Paul

O God,
who, through the preaching of the blessed Apostle Saint Paul,
hast caused the light of the Gospel
to shine throughout the world;
Grant, we beseech thee,
that we, having his wonderful conversion in remembrance,
may shew forth our thankfulness unto thee for the same,
by following the holy doctrine which he taught;
through Jesus Christ our Lord.

Almighty God,
who caused the light of the gospel
to shine throughout the world
through the preaching of your servant Saint Paul:
Grant that we who celebrate his wonderful conversion
may follow him in bearing witness to your truth;
through Jesus Christ our Lord. 1#

Gracious God,
you filled your apostle Paul with love for all the churches.
May this sacrament which we have received
foster love and unity among your people.
This we ask in the name of Jesus Christ our Lord. 16

Saint Brigid

Father,   COLLECT ONE
by the leadership of thy blessed servant Brigid
thou didst strengthen the Church in this land;
As we give thee thanks for her life of devoted service,
inspire us with new life and light,
and give us perseverance to serve thee all our days;
through Jesus Christ our Lord.

Father,   COLLECT TWO
by the leadership of your blessed servant Brigid
you strengthened the Church in this land:
As we give you thanks for her life of devoted service,
inspire us with new life and light,
and give us perseverance to serve you all our days;
through Jesus Christ our Lord. 2#

God of truth,   POST COMMUNION
whose Wisdom set her table and invited us to eat
the bread and drink the wine of the kingdom.
Help us to lay aside all foolishness
and to live and walk in the way of insight,
that in fellowship with all your saints
we may come to the eternal feast of heaven;
through Jesus Christ our Lord. 13#

Saint Patrick

O Almighty God,   COLLECT ONE
who in thy providence didst choose thy servant Patrick
to be the apostle of the Irish people,
that he might bring those
who were wandering in darkness and error
to the true light and knowledge of thee;
Grant us so to walk in that light,
that we may come at last to the light of everlasting life;
through the merits of Jesus Christ thy Son our Lord.

Almighty God,   COLLECT TWO
in your providence you chose your servant Patrick,
to be the apostle of the Irish people
to bring those who were wandering in darkness and error
to the true light and knowledge of your Word:
Grant that walking in that light
we may come at last to the light of everlasting life;
through Jesus Christ our Lord. I#

Hear us, most merciful God,   POST COMMUNION
for that part of the Church
which through your servant Patrick
you planted in our land;
that it may hold fast the faith entrusted to the saints
and in the end bear much fruit to eternal life:
through Jesus Christ our Lord. I#

Saint Joseph of Nazareth

O God, COLLECT ONE
who from the family of thy servant David
didst raise up Joseph to be the guardian of thine incarnate Son
and spouse of his virgin mother;
Give us grace to imitate his uprightness of life
and his obedience to thy commands:
through the same thy Son Jesus Christ our Lord. 6

God our Father, COLLECT TWO
who from the family of your servant David
raised up Joseph the carpenter
to be the guardian of your incarnate Son
and husband of the Blessed Virgin Mary:
Give us grace to follow his example
of faithful obedience to your commands;
through our Lord Jesus Christ,
who is alive and reigns with you and the Holy Spirit,
one God, now and for ever. 13#

Heavenly Father, POST COMMUNION
whose Son grew in wisdom and stature
in the home of Joseph the carpenter of Nazareth,
and on the wood of the cross perfected
the work of the world's salvation.
Help us, strengthened by this sacrament of his passion,
to count the wisdom of the world as foolishness,
and to walk with him in simplicity and trust;
through Jesus Christ our Lord. 13

The Annunciation of our Lord Jesus Christ to the Blessed Virgin Mary   *25 March*

We beseech thee, O Lord,   COLLECT ONE
pour thy grace into our hearts;
that, as we have known the Incarnation of thy Son Jesus Christ
by the message of an angel,
so by his cross and passion
we may be brought unto the glory of his resurrection;
through the same Jesus Christ our Lord.

Pour your grace into our hearts, Lord,   COLLECT TWO
that as we have known the incarnation of your Son Jesus Christ
by the message of an angel,
so by his cross and passion
we may be brought to the glory of his resurrection;
through Jesus Christ our Lord. 2

God Most High,   POST COMMUNION
whose handmaid bore the Word made flesh:
We thank you that in this sacrament of our redemption
you visit us with your Holy Spirit
and overshadow us by your power.
May we like Mary be joyful in our obedience,
and so bring forth the fruits of holiness;
through Jesus Christ our Lord. 8#

Saint Mark

O almighty God,   COLLECT ONE
who hast instructed thy holy Church
with the heavenly doctrine of thy evangelist Saint Mark;
Give us grace, that, being not like children
carried away with every blast of vain doctrine,
we may be established in the truth of thy holy Gospel;
through Jesus Christ our Lord.

Almighty God,   COLLECT TWO
who enlightened your holy Church
through the inspired witness of your evangelist Saint Mark:
Grant that we, being firmly grounded
in the truth of the gospel,
may be faithful to its teaching both in word and deed;
through Jesus Christ our Lord. 7

Blessed Lord,   POST COMMUNION
you have fed us at this table with sacramental gifts.
May we always rejoice and find strength
in the gift of the gospel
announced to us by Saint Mark,
and come at last to the fullness of everlasting life;
through Jesus Christ our Lord. 24

Saint Philip and Saint James

O almighty God,
COLLECT ONE
whom truly to know is everlasting life;
Grant us perfectly to know thy Son Jesus Christ
to be the way, the truth, and the life;
that, following in the steps of thy holy apostles,
Saint Philip and Saint James,
we may steadfastly walk in the way that leadeth to eternal life;
through the same thy Son Jesus Christ our Lord.

Almighty Father,
COLLECT TWO
whom truly to know is eternal life:
Teach us to know your Son Jesus Christ
as the way, the truth, and the life;
that we may follow the steps of your holy apostles
Philip and James,
and walk steadfastly in the way that leads to your glory;
through Jesus Christ our Lord. 1#

Holy God,
POST COMMUNION
in Jesus Christ we find the way to you.
May we, who have met him in this banquet,
be kept in your unending love,
and see you at work in your world,
through your Son, who is Lord for ever and ever. 16#

Saint Matthias

O almighty God,   COLLECT ONE
who into the place of the traitor Judas didst choose
thy faithful servant Matthias
to be of the number of the twelve apostles;
Grant that thy Church,
being alway preserved from false apostles,
may be ordered and guided by faithful and true pastors;
through Jesus Christ our Lord.

Almighty God,   COLLECT TWO
who in the place of the traitor Judas
chose your faithful servant Matthias
to be of the number of the Twelve:
Preserve your Church from false apostles
and, by the ministry of faithful pastors and teachers,
keep us steadfast in your truth;
through Jesus Christ our Lord. 1#

Lord God,   POST COMMUNION
the source of truth and love,
Keep us faithful to the apostles' teaching and fellowship,
united in prayer and the breaking of bread,
and one in joy and simplicity of heart,
in Jesus Christ our Lord. 13

Visitation of the Blessed Virgin Mary *31 May*

Almighty God,   COLLECT ONE
by whose grace Elizabeth rejoiced with Mary
and greeted her as the mother of the Lord;
Look with favour on thy lowly servants
that, with Mary, we may magnify thy holy name
and rejoice to acclaim her Son our Saviour,
who liveth and reigneth with thee and the Holy Spirit,
one God, now and for ever.

Mighty God,   COLLECT TWO
by whose grace Elizabeth rejoiced with Mary
and greeted her as the mother of the Lord:
Look with favour on your lowly servants
that, with Mary, we may magnify your holy name
and rejoice to acclaim her Son our Saviour,
who is alive and reigns with you and the Holy Spirit,
one God, now and for ever. 7#

Gracious God,   POST COMMUNION
who gave joy to Elizabeth and Mary
as they recognised the signs of redemption at work within them:
Help us, who have shared in the joy of this eucharist,
to know the Lord deep within us
and his love shining out in our lives,
that the world may rejoice in your salvation;
through Jesus Christ our Lord. 13

Saint Columba

9 June

O God, who didst call thy servant Columba COLLECT ONE
from among the princes of this land
to be a herald and evangelist of thy kingdom;
Grant that thy Church,
having his faith and courage in remembrance,
may so proclaim the splendour of thy grace,
that people everywhere will come to know thy Son
as their Saviour, and serve him as their King;
who liveth and reigneth with thee and the Holy Spirit,
one God, now and for ever.

O God, you called your servant Columba COLLECT TWO
from among the princes of this land
to be a herald and evangelist of your kingdom:
Grant that your Church, remembering his faith and courage,
may so proclaim the splendour of your grace
that people everywhere will come to know your Son
as their Saviour, and serve him as their King;
who lives and reigns with you and the Holy Spirit,
one God, now and for ever. 2

Lord Jesus, King of Saints, POST COMMUNION
you blessed Columba to find refuge in you
both at home and in exile.
May we, who have tasted your goodness at this table,
come with all your saints to the royal banquet
of your kingdom in heaven;
where with the Father and the Holy Spirit
you reign, for ever. 24

Saint Barnabas

O Lord God almighty,
who didst endue thy holy apostle Barnabas
with singular gifts of the Holy Spirit;
Leave us not, we beseech thee,
destitute of thy manifold gifts,
nor yet of grace to use them alway
to thy honour and glory;
through Jesus Christ our Lord.

Bountiful God, giver of all gifts,
who poured your Spirit upon your servant Barnabas:
Help us, by his example,
to be generous in all our judgements,
and unselfish in our service;
through Jesus Christ our Lord. 2#

Just and merciful God,
we have heard your word
and received new life at your table.
Kindle in us the flame of love
by which your apostle Barnabas bore witness to the gospel,
and send us out in Jesus' name
to encourage our brothers and sisters in faith.
We ask this for his sake. 24

The Birth of Saint John the Baptist *24 June*

Almighty God, COLLECT ONE
by whose providence thy servant John Baptist
was wonderfully born,
and sent to prepare the way of thy Son our Saviour,
by preaching of repentance;
Make us so to follow his doctrine and holy life,
that we may truly repent according to his preaching;
and after his example constantly speak the truth,
boldly rebuke vice, and patiently suffer for the truth's sake;
through Jesus Christ our Lord.

Almighty God, COLLECT TWO
by whose providence your servant John the Baptist
was wonderfully born,
and sent to prepare the way of your Son our Saviour,
by the preaching of repentance:
Lead us to repent according to his preaching,
and, after his example, constantly to speak the truth,
boldly to rebuke vice, and patiently to suffer for the truth's sake;
through Jesus Christ our Lord. 1#

Merciful Lord, POST COMMUNION
whose prophet John the Baptist
proclaimed your Son as the Lamb of God
who takes away the sin of the world:
Grant, that we who in this sacrament have known
your forgiveness and your life-giving love,
may ever tell of your mercy and your peace;
through Jesus Christ our Lord. 13

Saint Peter 29 June

O almighty God, COLLECT ONE
who by thy Son Jesus Christ didst give
to thy apostle Saint Peter many excellent gifts,
and commandedst him earnestly to feed thy flock;
Make, we beseech thee, all bishops and pastors
diligently to preach thy holy Word,
and the people obediently to follow the same,
that they may receive the crown of everlasting glory;
through Jesus Christ our Lord

Almighty God, COLLECT TWO
who inspired your apostle Saint Peter
to confess Jesus as Christ and Son of the living God:
Build up your Church upon this rock,
that in unity and peace it may proclaim one truth
and follow one Lord, your Son our Saviour Christ,
who is alive and reigns with you and the Holy Spirit,
one God, now and for ever. 1#

Heavenly Father, POST COMMUNION
ever renew the life of your Church
by the power of this sacrament.
Keep us united in your love
through the teaching of the apostles and the breaking of bread,
in the name of Jesus Christ the Lord. 16#

Saint Thomas

Almighty and everliving God,

who, for the more confirmation of the faith
didst suffer thy holy apostle Thomas
to be doubtful of thy Son's resurrection;
Grant us so perfectly, and without all doubt,
to believe in thy Son Jesus Christ,
that our faith in thy sight may never be reproved.
Hear us, O Lord, through the same Jesus Christ,
to whom, with thee and the Holy Spirit,
be all honour and glory, now and for evermore

Almighty and eternal God,

who, for the firmer foundation of our faith,
allowed your holy apostle Thomas
to doubt the resurrection of your Son
till word and sight convinced him:
Grant to us, who have not seen,
that we also may believe
and so confess Christ as our Lord and our God;
who is alive and reigns with you and the Holy Spirit,
one God, now and for ever. 7#

God of hope,

in this eucharist we have tasted
the promise of your heavenly banquet
and the richness of eternal life.
May we who bear witness to the death of your Son,
also proclaim the glory of his resurrection,
for he is Lord for ever and ever. 16

Saint Mary Magdalene   *22 July*

Almighty God,   COLLECT ONE
whose blessed Son restored Mary Magdalene
to health of body and mind,
and called her to be a witness to his resurrection;
Mercifully grant that by thy grace
we may healed of our infirmities
and know thee in the power of his endless life;
who with thee and the Holy Spirit,
liveth and reigneth one God, now and for ever. 6

Almighty God,   COLLECT TWO
whose Son restored Mary Magdalene
to health of mind and body
and called her to be a witness to his resurrection:
Forgive our sins and heal us by your grace,
that we may serve you in the power of his risen life;
who is alive and reigns with you and the Holy Spirit,
one God, now and for ever. 7#

God of life and love,   POST COMMUNION
whose risen Son called Mary Magdalene by name
and sent her to tell of his resurrection to his apostles:
In your mercy, help us,
who have been united with him in this eucharist,
to proclaim the good news
that he is alive and reigns with you and the Holy Spirit,
one God, now and for ever. 13

Saint James the Apostle

Grant, O merciful God,
that as thine holy apostle Saint James,
leaving his father and all that he had,
without delay was obedient unto the calling
of thy Son Jesus Christ, and followed him;
so we, forsaking all worldly and carnal affections,
may be evermore ready to follow thy holy commandments;
through Jesus Christ our Lord.

Merciful God,
whose holy apostle Saint James,
leaving his father and all that he had,
was obedient to the calling of your Son Jesus Christ
and followed him even to death:
Help us, forsaking the false attractions of the world,
to be ready at all times to answer your call without delay;
through Jesus Christ our Lord. 1#

Father,
we have eaten at your table
and drunk from the cup of your kingdom.
Teach us the way of service
that in compassion and humility
we may reflect the glory of Jesus Christ,
Son of Man and Son of God, our Lord. 16

The Transfiguration of our Lord   *6 August*

O almighty God,   COLLECT ONE
whose only-begotten Son was transfigured
before chosen witnesses on the holy mount,
and amidst the exceeding glory spake of his decease
which he should accomplish at Jerusalem;
Grant to us thy servants
that, beholding the brightness of his countenance,
we may be strengthened to bear our cross;
through the same Jesus Christ our Lord.

Father in heaven,   COLLECT TWO
whose Son Jesus Christ was wonderfully transfigured
before chosen witnesses upon the holy mountain,
and spoke of the exodus he would accomplish at Jerusalem:
Give us strength so to hear his voice
and bear our cross in this world,
that in the world to come we may see him as he is;
where he is alive and reigns with you and the Holy Spirit,
one God, now and for ever. 2#

Holy God,   POST COMMUNION
we see your glory in the face of Jesus Christ.
May we who are partakers at his table
reflect his life in word and deed,
that all the world may know
his power to change and save.
This we ask through Jesus Christ our Lord. 16#

Saint Bartholomew

O almighty and everlasting God,
who didst give to thine apostle Bartholomew
grace truly to believe and to preach thy Word;
Grant, we beseech thee, unto thy Church,
to love that Word which he believed,
and both to preach and receive the same;
through Jesus Christ our Lord.

Almighty and everlasting God,
who gave to your apostle Bartholomew
grace truly to believe and to preach your word:
Grant that your Church
may love that word which he believed
and may faithfully preach and receive the same;
through Jesus Christ our Lord. 1#

God of our salvation,
you have fed us at the table of your Son Jesus Christ our Lord.
Lead us in his way of service,
that your kingdom may be known on earth,
your saving power among all nations.
Grant this for his name's sake. 16#

The Birth of the Blessed Virgin Mary 8 *September*

Almighty God,
who didst look upon the lowliness of the blessed Virgin Mary
and didst choose her to be the mother of thine only Son;
Grant that we, who are redeemed by his blood,
may share with her in the glory of thine eternal kingdom;
through Jesus Christ our Lord.

Almighty God,
who looked upon the lowliness of the blessed Virgin Mary
and chose her to be the mother of your only Son:
Grant that we who are redeemed by his blood
may share with her in the glory of your eternal kingdom;
through Jesus Christ our Lord. 7

Almighty and everlasting God,
who stooped to raise fallen humanity
through the child-bearing of blessed Mary:
Grant that we who have seen your glory
revealed in our human nature,
and your love made perfect in our weakness,
may daily be renewed in your image,
and conformed to the pattern of your Son,
Jesus Christ our Lord. 8

Saint Matthew

O almighty God, COLLECT ONE
who by thy blessed Son didst call Matthew
from the receipt of custom to be an apostle and evangelist;
Grant us grace to forsake all covetous desires,
and inordinate love of riches,
and to follow the same thy Son Jesus Christ,
who liveth and reigneth with thee and the Holy Spirit,
one God, now and for ever.

O almighty God, COLLECT TWO
whose blessed Son called Matthew the tax-collector
to be an apostle and evangelist:
Give us grace to forsake the selfish pursuit of gain
and the possessive love of riches;
that we may follow in the way of your Son Jesus Christ,
who is alive and reigns with you and the Holy Spirit,
one God, now and for ever. 1#

God of mercy and compassion, POST COMMUNION
we have shared the joy of salvation
that Matthew knew when Jesus called him.
Renew our calling to proclaim the one
who came not to call the righteous but sinners to salvation,
your Son Jesus Christ our Lord. 16#

Saint Michael and all Angels *29 September*

O everlasting God, COLLECT ONE
who hast ordained and constituted
the services of angels and men in a wonderful order;
Mercifully grant, that as thy holy angels alway
do thee service in heaven,
so, by thy appointment,
they may succour and defend us on earth;
through Jesus Christ our Lord.

Everlasting God, COLLECT TWO
you have ordained and constituted the ministries
of angels and mortals in a wonderful order:
Grant that as your holy angels always serve you in heaven,
so, at your command,
they may help and defend us on earth;
through Jesus Christ our Lord. 1#

Lord of heaven, POST COMMUNION
in this eucharist you have brought us near
to an innumerable company of angels
and to the spirits of the saints made perfect.
As in this food of our earthly pilgrimage
we have shared their fellowship,
so may we come to share their joy in heaven;
through Jesus Christ our Lord. 8

Saint Philip the Deacon *11 October*

Lord God, <small>COLLECT ONE</small>
whose Spirit didst guide Philip the deacon
to show how ancient prophecies are fulfilled in Jesus Christ;
Open our minds to understand the Scriptures,
and deepen our faith in him;
who liveth and reigneth with thee and the Holy Spirit,
one God, for ever and ever. 3

Lord God, <small>COLLECT TWO</small>
your Spirit guided Philip the deacon
to show how ancient prophecies are fulfilled in Jesus Christ:
Open our minds to understand the Scriptures,
and deepen our faith in him;
who is alive and reigns with you and the Holy Spirit,
one God, for ever and ever. 3

We thank you, Lord, that you call and use <small>POST COMMUNION</small>
people with different gifts to build your kingdom.
May we, who are strengthened by this sacrament,
like Philip and his family rejoice to serve you
by the witness of our lives and homes;
though Jesus Christ our Lord. 24

Saint Luke

Almighty God,
who calledst Luke the physician,
whose praise is in the gospel,
to be an evangelist, and physician of the soul;
May it please thee, that by the wholesome medicines
of the doctrine delivered by him,
all the diseases of our souls may be healed;
through the merits of thy Son Jesus Christ our Lord.

COLLECT ONE

Almighty God,
you called Luke the physician,
whose praise is in the gospel,
to be an evangelist and physician of the soul:
By the grace of the Spirit
and through the wholesome medicine of the gospel,
give your Church the same love and power to heal;
through Jesus Christ our Lord. 1#

COLLECT TWO

Living God,
may we who have shared these holy mysteries
enjoy health of body and mind
and witness faithfully to your gospel,
in the name of Jesus Christ our Lord. 16

POST COMMUNION

Saint James, the brother of our Lord   *23 October*

Grant, we beseech thee, O God,   Collect One
that after the example of thy servant, James the Just,
brother of our Lord,
thy Church may give itself continually to prayer
and to the reconciliation of all who are at variance and enmity;
through Jesus Christ our Lord. 6

Lord, God of peace: Collect Two
Grant that after the example of your servant,
James the brother of our Lord,
your Church may give itself continually to prayer
and to the reconciliation of all
who are caught up in hatred or enmity;
through Jesus Christ our Lord. 3

Lord Jesus Christ,   Post Communion
we thank you that after your resurrection you appeared to James,
and endowed him with gifts of leadership for your Church.
May we, who have known you now in the breaking of bread,
be people of prayer and reconciliation.
We ask it for your love's sake.

Saint Simon and Saint Jude

O almighty God,   COLLECT ONE
who hast built thy Church upon the foundation
of the apostles and prophets,
Jesus Christ himself being the head corner-stone;
Grant us so to be joined together
in unity of spirit by their doctrine,
that we may be made an holy temple acceptable unto thee;
through Jesus Christ our Lord.

Almighty God,   COLLECT TWO
who built your Church upon the foundation
of the apostles and prophets
with Jesus Christ himself as the chief corner-stone:
So join us together in unity of spirit by their doctrine
that we may be made a holy temple acceptable to you;
through Jesus Christ our Lord. 1#

Lord God,   POST COMMUNION
the source of truth and love:
Keep us faithful to the apostles' teaching and fellowship,
united in prayer and the breaking of bread,
and one in joy and simplicity of heart,
in Jesus Christ our Lord. 13

All Saints' Day

May be observed on the nearest Sunday.

O almighty God,   COLLECT ONE
who hast knit together thine elect
in one communion and fellowship,
in the mystical body of thy Son Christ our Lord;
Grant us so to follow thy blessed saints
in all virtuous and godly living,
that we may come to those unspeakable joys,
which thou hast prepared for them that unfeignedly love thee;
through Jesus Christ our Lord.

Almighty God,   COLLECT TWO
you have knit together your elect
in one communion and fellowship
in the mystical body of your Son Christ our Lord:
Grant us grace so to follow your blessed saints
in all virtuous and godly living
that we may come to those inexpressible joys
that you have prepared for those who truly love you;
through Jesus Christ our Lord. 1#

God, the source of all holiness   POST COMMUNION
and giver of all good things:
May we who have shared at this table
as strangers and pilgrims here on earth
be welcomed with all your saints
to the heavenly feast on the day of your kingdom;
through Jesus Christ our Lord. 8

Saint Andrew

Almighty God, COLLECT ONE
who didst give such grace unto thy holy apostle Saint Andrew,
that he readily obeyed the calling of thy Son Jesus Christ,
and followed him without delay;
Grant unto us all, that we being called by thy holy Word,
may forthwith give up ourselves obediently
to fulfil thy holy commandments;
through the same Jesus Christ our Lord.

Almighty God, COLLECT TWO
who gave such grace to your apostle Saint Andrew
that he readily obeyed the call of your Son Jesus Christ
and brought his brother with him:
Call us by your holy Word
and give us grace to follow without delay,
and to tell the good news of your kingdom;
through Jesus Christ our Lord. 2#

Father, POST COMMUNION
May the gifts we have received at your table
keep us alert for your call
that we may always be ready to answer,
and, following the example of Saint Andrew,
always be ready to bear our witness
to our Saviour Jesus Christ. 24

Saint Stephen

Grant, O Lord,
that in all our sufferings here upon earth
for the testimony of thy truth,
we may steadfastly look up to heaven,
and by faith behold the glory that shall be revealed;
and, being filled with the Holy Spirit,
may learn to love and bless our persecutors
by the example of thy first martyr Saint Stephen,
who prayed for his murderers to thee,
O blessed Jesus, who standest at the right hand of God
to succour all those that suffer for thee,
our only Mediator and Advocate.

Gracious Father,
who gave the first martyr Stephen
grace to pray for those who stoned him:
Grant that in all our sufferings for the truth
we may learn to love even our enemies
and to seek forgiveness for those who desire our hurt,
looking up to heaven to him who was crucified for us,
Jesus Christ, our Mediator and Advocate,
who is alive and reigns with you and the Holy Spirit,
one God, now and for ever. 1#

Merciful Lord,
we thank you for these signs of your mercy,
we praise you for feeding us at your table
and giving us joy in honouring Stephen,
first martyr of the new Israel;
through Jesus Christ our Lord. 14#

Saint John the Evangelist

27 December

Merciful Lord, COLLECT ONE
we beseech thee to cast thy bright beams of light
upon thy Church,
that it, being enlightened by the doctrine
of thy blessed apostle and evangelist Saint John,
may so walk in the light of thy truth,
that it may at length attain to the light of everlasting life;
through Jesus Christ our Lord.

Merciful Lord, COLLECT TWO
Cast your bright beams of light upon the Church;
that, being enlightened by the teaching
of your blessed apostle and evangelist Saint John,
we may so walk in the light of your truth
that we may at last attain to the light of everlasting life
through Jesus Christ your incarnate Son our Lord. 1#

Grant, O Lord, we pray, POST COMMUNION
that the Word made flesh proclaimed by your apostle John
may ever abide and live within us;
through Jesus Christ our Lord. 20

Saint John the Evangelist **123**

The Holy Innocents

O almighty God,   COLLECT ONE
who out of the mouths of babes and sucklings
hast ordained strength,
and madest infants to glorify thee by their deaths:
Mortify and kill all vices in us,
and so strengthen us by thy grace,
that by the innocency of our lives,
and constancy of our faith even unto death,
we may glorify thy holy Name;
through Jesus Christ our Lord.

Heavenly Father,   COLLECT TWO
whose children suffered at the hands of Herod:
By your great might frustrate all evil designs,
and establish your reign of justice, love and peace;
through Jesus Christ our Lord. 16#

Eternal God,   POST COMMUNION
comfort of the afflicted and healer of the broken,
you have fed us this day at the table of life and hope.
Teach us the ways of gentleness and peace,
that all the world may acknowledge
the kingdom of your Son Jesus Christ our Lord. 16

Special Occasions

Dedication Festival

O almighty God,   COLLECT ONE
to whose glory we celebrate the dedication of this house of prayer;
We praise thee for the many blessings
thou hast given to those who worship here,
and we pray that all who seek thee in this place
may find thee, and, being filled with the Holy Spirit,
may become a living temple acceptable to thee;
through Jesus Christ our Lord.

Almighty God,   COLLECT TWO
to whose glory we celebrate the dedication of this house of prayer:
We praise you for the many blessings
you have given to those who worship here,
and we pray that all who seek you in this place
may find you, and, being filled with the Holy Spirit,
may become a living temple acceptable to you
through Jesus Christ our Lord. 2

Father in heaven,   POST COMMUNION
your church on earth is a sign of heavenly peace,
an image of the new and eternal Jerusalem.
Grant to us in the days of our pilgrimage
that, fed with the living bread of heaven,
and united in the body of your Son,
we may become the temple of your presence,
the place of your glory on earth,
and a sign of your peace in the world;
through Jesus Christ our Lord. 13

Harvest Thanksgiving

O almighty and everlasting God,   COLLECT ONE
who hast graciously given unto us
the fruits of the earth in their season;
We yield thee humble and hearty thanks for this thy bounty;
beseeching thee to give us grace rightly
to use the same to thy glory,
and the relief of those that need;
through Jesus Christ our Lord,
who liveth and reigneth with thee and the Holy Spirit,
one God, world without end.

or

O almighty God and heavenly Father;
We glorify thee that thou hast fulfilled to us thy gracious promise,
that, while the earth remaineth,
seed-time and harvest shall not fail.
We bless thee for the kindly fruits of the earth,
which thou hast given to our use.
Teach us, we beseech thee, to remember
that it is not by bread alone that man doth live;
and grant us evermore to feed on him
who is the true bread form heaven,
Jesus Christ our Lord,
to whom with thee and the Holy Spirit,
be all honour and glory, world without end.

Eternal God,
you crown the year with your goodness
and give us the fruits of the earth in their season:
Grant that we may use them to your glory,
for the relief of those in need
and for our own well-being;
through Jesus Christ our Lord. 1#

Lord of the harvest,
with joy we have offered thanksgiving
for your love in creation
and have shared in the bread and wine of the kingdom.
By your grace plant within us such reverence
for all that you give us
that will make us wise stewards of the good things we enjoy;
through Jesus Christ our Lord. 13

The Guidance of the Holy Spirit

For the Opening of a Synod

God,   COLLECT ONE

who didst teach the hearts of thy faithful people,
by the sending to them the light of thy Holy Spirit;
Grant us by the same Spirit to have a right judgement in all things,
and evermore to rejoice in his holy comfort;
through the merits of Christ Jesus our Saviour,
who liveth and reigneth with thee,
in the unity of the same Spirit, one God, world without end.

God,   COLLECT TWO

who from of old
taught the hearts of your faithful people
by sending to them the light of your Holy Spirit:
Grant us by the same Spirit to have a right judgement in all things
and evermore to rejoice in his holy comfort;
through the merits of Christ Jesus our Saviour,
who is alive and reigns with you in the unity of the Spirit,
one God, now and for ever. 1 #

or

Almighty God,
you have given your Holy Spirit to the Church
to lead us into all truth:
Bless with the Spirit's grace and presence
the members of this ... *(synod/vestry/etc);*
keep *us/them* steadfast in faith and united in love,
that *we/they* may manifest your glory
and prepare the way of your kingdom;
through Jesus Christ our Lord. 7#

God of power,
whose Holy Spirit renews your people
in the bread and wine we bless and share:
May the boldness of the Spirit transform us,
the gentleness of the Spirit lead us,
and the gifts of the Spirit equip us
to serve and worship you;
through Jesus Christ our Lord. 22#

Ember Days: Ministry

For the ministry of all Christian people

Almighty and everlasting God, COLLECT
by whose Spirit the whole body of the Church
is governed and sanctified:
Hear our prayer which we offer for all your faithful people,
that in their vocation and ministry
they may serve you in holiness and truth
to the glory of your name;
through our Lord and Saviour Jesus Christ. 1#

For those to be ordained

Almighty God, the giver of all good gifts, COLLECT
by your Holy Spirit you have appointed
various orders of ministry in the Church:
Look with mercy on your *servant(s)* now called to be
deacons / priests / a bishop;
maintain *them* in truth and renew *them* in holiness,
that by word and good example *they* may faithfully serve you
to the glory of your name
and the benefit of your Church;
through the merits of our Saviour Jesus Christ. 1#
The words in italics are varied as required.

For vocations to Holy Orders

Almighty God,
you have entrusted to your Church
a share in the ministry of your Son our great High Priest:
Inspire by your Holy Spirit the hearts of many
to offer themselves for ordination in your Church,
that strengthened by his power,
they may work for the increase of your kingdom
and set forward the eternal praise of your name;
through Jesus Christ our Lord. 2#

For the inauguration of a new ministry

God our Father, Lord of all the world,   COLLECT
through your Son you have called us into the fellowship
of your universal Church:
Hear our prayer for your faithful people
that in their vocation and ministry
each may be an instrument of your love,
and give to your servant ... now to be ... *installed,/ instituted, / ....*
the needful gifts of grace;
through our Lord and Saviour Jesus Christ.

Heavenly Father,   POST COMMUNION
whose ascended Son gave gifts of leadership
and service to the Church:
Strengthen us who have received this holy food
to be good stewards of your manifold grace;
through him who came not to be served but to serve,
and give his life as a ransom for many,
Jesus Christ our Lord. 13

or

Lord of the harvest,
you have fed your people in this sacrament
with the fruits of creation made holy by your Spirit.
By your grace raise up among us faithful labourers
to sow your word and reap the harvest of souls;
through Jesus Christ our Lord. 10#

Rogation Days

Almighty God,
whose will it is that the earth and the sea
should bear fruit in due season:
Bless the labours of those who work on land and sea,
grant us a good harvest
and the grace always to rejoice in your fatherly care;
through Jesus Christ our Lord. 23#

or

Almighty God and Father,
you have so ordered our life
that we are dependent on one another:
Prosper those engaged in commerce and industry
and direct their minds and hands
that they may rightly use your gifts in the service of others;
through Jesus Christ our Lord. 23

God our creator,
you give seed for us to sow and bread for us to eat.
As you have blessed the fruit of our labour in this eucharist,
so we ask you to give all your children their daily bread,
that the world may praise you for your goodness;
through Jesus Christ our Lord. 22#

Mission

Almighty God,
who called your Church to witness
that you were in Christ reconciling the world to yourself:
Help us to proclaim the good news of your love,
that all who hear it may be drawn to you;
through him who was lifted up on the cross,
and reigns with you and the Holy Spirit,
one God, now and for ever. 2#

Eternal Giver of love and power,   POST COMMUNION
your Son Jesus Christ has sent us into all the world
to preach the gospel of his kingdom.
Confirm us in this mission,
and help us to live the good news we proclaim;
through Jesus Christ our Lord. 16

Peace

Almighty God,
from whom all thoughts of truth and peace proceed:
Kindle, we pray, in every heart the true love of peace;
and guide with your pure and peaceable wisdom
those who take counsel for the nations of the earth,
that in tranquillity your kingdom may go forward,
till the earth is filled with the knowledge of your love;
through Jesus Christ our Lord. 1#

God our Father,
your Son is our peace
and his cross the sign of reconciliation.
Help us, who share the broken bread,
to bring together what is scattered
and to bind up what is wounded,
that Christ may bring in the everlasting kingdom of his peace;
who is alive and reigns with you and the Holy Spirit,
one God, now and for ever. 13

Unity

Heavenly Father, COLLECT
you have called us in the body of your Son Jesus Christ
to continue his work of reconciliation
and reveal you to the world:
forgive us the sins which tear us apart;
give us the courage to overcome our fears
and to seek that unity which is your gift and your will;
through Jesus Christ our Lord. 7#

or

Lord Jesus Christ,
who said to your apostles,
Peace I leave with you, my peace I give to you:
look not on our sins but on the faith of your Church,
and grant it the peace and unity of your kingdom;
where you are alive and reign with the Father
and the Holy Spirit, one God, now and for ever. 1#

Eternal God and Father, POST COMMUNION
whose Son at supper prayed that his disciples might be one,
as he is one with you:
Draw us closer to him,
that in common love and obedience to you
we may be united to one another
in the fellowship of the one Spirit,
that the world may believe that he is Lord,
to your eternal glory;
through Jesus Christ our Lord. 8#

Bible Sunday

Blessed Lord,
who caused all holy scriptures to be written for our learning:
help us to hear them,
to read, mark, learn and inwardly digest them
that, through patience, and the comfort of your holy word,
we may embrace and for ever hold fast
the hope of everlasting life,
which you have given us in our Saviour Jesus Christ. 1#

God of all grace,   POST COMMUNION
your Son Jesus Christ fed the hungry
with the bread of his life
and the word of his kingdom.
Renew your people with your heavenly grace,
and in all our weakness
sustain us by your true and living bread,
who is alive and reigns with you and the Holy Spirit,
one God, now and for ever. 16#

Prayers are from the following sources:

1	*Book of Common Prayer*, Church of Ireland 1926, 1933, 1962
2	*Alternative Prayer Book*, Church of Ireland 1984
3	*An Anglican Prayer Book*, Church of Southern Africa 1989
4	*Book of Common Prayer*, Church in Wales 1984
5	*A Prayer Book for Australia*, 1978
6	*Book of Common Prayer*, Episcopal Church of the USA 1979
7	*Alternative Service Book*, Church of England 1980
8	*Promise of His Glory*, Church of England 1990
9	*Lent, Holy Week and Easter*, Church of England 1988
10	*After Communion*, Charles MacDonnell, Mowbray 1985
11	Original prayer by Kenneth Stevenson
12	Original prayer by David Silk
13	*Common Worship*, Church of England 2000
14	Original prayer by members of Inter Provincial Consultation
15	*Celebrating Common Prayer*, Society of Saint Francis 1992
16	*Book of Alternative Services*, Anglican Church of Canada 1986
17	Prayer in use at Westcott House, Cambridge
18	*Enriching the Christian Year*, Alcuin Club / SPCK 1993
19	*Patterns for Worship*, Church of England 1995
20	Material prepared by International Commission on English in the Liturgy (ICEL)
21	Prayer ascribed to Thomas Aquinas from *Missale Romanum*
22	Original prayer by Janet Morley
23	*A New Zealand Prayer Book*, 1988
24	Original prayer by Brian Mayne

See the acknowledgment of copyright permissions on page 4

A Table of Epistles and Gospels

Drawn from those appointed in the Book of Common Prayer 1926
which may be used at Holy Communion with Collects One.

Advent 1	Romans 13: 8-14	Matthew 21: 1-13
Advent 2	Romans 15: 4-13	Luke 21: 25-33
Advent 3	1 Corinthians 4: 1-5	Matthew 11: 2-11
Advent 4	Philippians 4: 4-7	John 1: 19-28

CHRISTMAS

Nativity (night)	Titus 2: 11-14	Matthew 1: 18-25
Nativity (day)	Hebrews 1: 1-12	John 1: 1-14
Christmas 1	Galatians 4: 1-7	Matthew 1: 18-25
Christmas 2	1 John 4: 9-16	John 1: 14-18

EPIPHANY

Epiphany	Ephesians 3: 1-12	Matthew 2: 1-12
Epiphany 1	Romans 12: 1-5	Luke 2: 41-52
Epiphany 2	Romans 12: 6-16a	John 2: 1-11
Epiphany 3	Romans 12: 16b-21	Matthew 8: 1-13
Epiphany 4	Romans 13: 1-7	Matthew 8: 23-34

BEFORE LENT

5 before Lent	Colossians 3: 12-17	Matthew 13: 24-30
4 before Lent	1 Corinthians 9: 24-27	Matthew 20: 1-16
3 before Lent	1 John 4: 1-6	John 3: 16-21
2 before Lent	2 Corinthians 11: 19-31	Luke 8: 4-15
1 before Lent	1 Corinthians 13: 1-13	Luke 18: 31-43

LENT

Ash Wednesday	Joel 2: 12-17	Matthew 6: 16-21
Lent 1	2 Corinthians 6: 1-10	Matthew 4: 1-11
Lent 2	1 Thessalonians 4: 1-8	Matthew 15: 21-28
Lent 3	Ephesians 5: 1-14	Luke 11: 14-28

Lent 4	Galatians 4: 21-31	John 6: 1-14
Lent 5	Hebrews 9: 11-15	John 8: 46-59a
Lent 6	Philippians 2: 5-11	Matthew 27: 1-54
Monday in Holy Week	Isaiah 63: 1-19	Mark 14: 1-72
Tuesday in Holy Week	Isaiah 50: 5-11	Mark 15: 1-39
Wednes. in Holy Week	Hebrews 9: 16-28	Luke 22: 1-71
Maundy Thursday	1 Corinthians 11: 23-34	Luke 23: 1-49
Good Friday	Hebrews 10: 1-25	John 19: 1-37
Easter Eve	1 Peter 3: 17-22	Matthew 27: 57-66

EASTER

Easter Day	Colossians 3: 1-7	John 20: 1-10
(A first service)	Hebrews 13: 20-21	Mark 16: 1-8
Monday:	Acts 10: 34-43	Luke 24: 13-35
Tuesday:	Acts 13: 26-41	Luke 24: 36-48
Easter 2	1 Corinthians 5: 6-8	John 20: 19-23
Easter 3	1 Peter 2: 19-25	John 10: 11-16
Easter 4	1 Peter 2: 11-17	John 16: 16-22
Easter 5	James 1: 17-21	John 16: 5-14
Easter 6	James 1: 22-27	John 16: 23-33
Ascension Day	Acts 1: 1-11	Mark 16: 14-20
Easter 71	Peter 4: 7-11	John 15:26 - 16:4b
Pentecost	Acts 2: 1-11	John 14: 15-31b

AFTER PENTECOST AND BEFORE ADVENT

| Monday | Acts 10: 34-48 | John 3: 16-21 |
| or Tuesday | Acts 8: 14-17 | John 10: 1-10 |

Trinity Sunday	Revelation 4: 1-11	John 3: 1-15
Trinity 1	1 John 4: 7-21	Luke 16: 19-31
Trinity 2	1 John 3: 13-24	Luke 14: 16b-24
Trinity 3	1 Peter 5: 5-14	Luke 15: 1-10
Trinity 4	Romans 8: 18-23	Luke 6: 36-42
Trinity 5	1 Peter 3: 8-15a	Luke 5: 1-11
Trinity 6	Romans 6: 3-11	Matthew 5: 20-26
Trinity 7	Romans 6: 19-23	Mark 8: 1-9

Trinity 8	Romans 8: 12-17	Matthew 7: 15-21
Trinity 9	1 Corinthians 10: 1-13	Luke 16: 1-9
Trinity 10	1 Corinthians 12: 1-11	Luke 19: 41-47a
Trinity 11	1 Corinthians 15: 1-11	Luke 18: 9-14
Trinity 12	2 Corinthians 3: 4-9	Mark 7: 31-37
Trinity 13	Galatians 3: 16-22	Luke 10: 23-27
Trinity 14	Galatians 5: 16-24	Luke 17: 11-19
Trinity 15	Galatians 6: 11-18	Matthew 6: 24-34
Trinity 16	Ephesians 3: 13-21	Luke 7: 11-17
Trinity 17	Ephesians 4: 1-6	Luke 14: 1-11
Trinity 18	1 Corinthians 1: 4-8	Matthew 22: 34-46
Trinity 19	Ephesians 4: 17-32	Matthew 9: 1-8
Trinity 20	Ephesians 5: 15-21	Matthew 22: 1-14
Trinity 21	Ephesians 6: 10-20	John 4: 46-54
5 before Advent	Philippians 1: 3-11	Matthew 18: 21-35
4 before Advent	Philippians 3: 17-21	Matthew 22: 15-22
3 before Advent	Colossians 1: 3-12	Matthew 9: 18-26
2 before Advent	1 John 3: 1-8	Matthew 24: 23-31
1 before Advent	Jeremiah 23: 5-8	John 6: 5-14

Naming & Circumcision	Ephesians 2: 11-18	Luke 2: 15-21
Conversion of St Paul	Acts 9: 1-22	Matthew 19: 27-30
St Brigid	1 John 1: 1-4	John 10: 7-16
Presentation	Malachi 3: 1-5	Luke 2: 22-40
St Patrick	Revelation 22: 1-5	Matthew 10: 16-23
St Joseph	2 Samuel 7: 4, 8-16	Luke 2: 41-52
Annunciation	Isaiah 7: 10-15	Luke 1: 26-38
St Mark	Ephesians 4: 7-16	John 15: 1-11
St Philip & St James	James 1: 1-12	John 14: 1-14
St Matthias	Acts 1: 15-26	Matthew 11: 25-30
Visitation	Romans 12: 9-16b	Luke 1: 39-47
St Columba	2 Corinthians 4: 5-11	Matthew 28: 16-20
St Barnabas	Acts 11: 22-30	John 15: 12-16
Birth of John Baptist	Isaiah 40: 1-11	Luke 1: 57-80
St Peter	Acts 12: 1-11	Matthew 16: 13-19

St Thomas	Ephesians 2: 19-22	John 20: 19-29
St Mary Magdalene	2 Corinthians 5: 14-18	John 20: 1-3, 11-18
St James	Acts 11: 27 - 12: 3a	Matthew 20: 20-28
Transfiguration	2 Peter 1: 12-18	Luke 9: 28-36
St Bartholomew	Acts 5: 12-16	Luke 22: 24-30
Birth of BVM	Isaiah 7: 10-15	Luke 1: 46-55 or Luke 2: 1-7
St Matthew	2 Corinthians 4: 1-6	Matthew 9: 9-13
St Michael & All Angels	Revelation 12: 7-12	Matthew 18: 1-10
St Philip the Deacon	Acts 8: 26-40	Matthew 13: 47-52
St Luke	2 Timothy 4: 5-15	Luke 10: 1-7a
St James of Jerusalem	Acts 15: 12-22a	Matthew 13: 54-58
St Simon & St Jude	Jude 1-8	John 17: 17-27
All Saints' Day	Revelation 7: 2-12	Matthew 5: 1-12
St Andrew	Romans 10: 9-21	Matthew 4: 18-22
St Stephen	Acts 7: 56-60	Matthew 23: 34-39
St John	1 John 1: 1-10	John 21: 19-25
Holy Innocents	Revelation 14: 1-5	Matthew 2: 13-18

Dates of Easter 2001 - 2030

The Date of Easter and Other Variable Dates

Year	Ash Wednesday	Easter Day	Ascension Day	Pentecost	Advent 1
2001	28 Feb	15 April	24 May	3 June	2 Dec
2002	13 Feb	31 March	9 May	19 May	1 Dec
2003	5 March	20 April	29 May	8 June	30 Nov
2004	25 Feb	11 April	20 May	30 May	28 Nov
2005	9 Feb	27 March	5 May	15 May	27 Nov
2006	1 March	16 April	25 May	4 June	3 Dec
2007	21 Feb	8 April	17 May	27 May	2 Dec
2008	6 Feb	23 March	1 May	11 May	30 Nov
2009	25 Feb	12 April	21 May	31 May	29 Nov
2010	17 Feb	4 April	13 May	23 May	28 Nov
2011	9 March	24 April	2 June	12 June	27 Nov
2012	22 Feb	8 April	17 May	27 May	2 Dec
2013	13 Feb	31 March	9 May	19 May	1 Dec
2014	5 March	20 April	29 May	8 June	30 Nov
2015	18 Feb	5 April	14 May	24 May	29 Nov
2016	10 Feb	27 March	5 May	15 May	27 Nov
2017	1 March	16 April	25 May	4 June	3 Dec
2018	14 Feb	1 April	10 May	20 May	2 Dec
2019	6 March	21 April	30 May	9 June	1 Dec
2020	26 Feb	12 April	21 May	31 May	29 Nov
2021	17 Feb	4 April	13 May	23 May	28 Nov
2022	2 March	17 April	26 May	5 June	27 Nov
2023	22 Feb	9 April	18 May	28 May	3 Dec
2024	14 Feb	31 March	9 May	19 May	1 Dec
2025	5 March	20 April	29 May	8 June	30 Nov
2026	18 Feb	5 April	14 May	24 May	29 Nov
2027	10 Feb	28 March	6 May	16 May	28 Nov
2028	1 March	16 April	25 May	4 June	3 Dec
2029	14 Feb	1 April	10 May	20 May	2 Dec
2030	6 March	21 April	30 May	9 June	1 Dec